What I Need You To Know

A Young Girl's Journal on Being Homeless

Written and illustrated by
Elizabeth A. Terrell

WORKBOOK PRESS LLC

187 E Warm Springs Rd,

Suite B285 Las Vegas NV 89119 USA

Website: https://workbookpress.com/

Hotline: 1-888-818-4856

Email: admin@workbookpress.com

Ordering Information:

Quantity sales. Special discounts are available on quantity purchases by corporations, associations, and others. For details, contact the publisher at the address above.

Library of Congress Control Number:

ISBN-13:   978-1-965732-83-0   Paperback Version

REV. DATE: 6/27/2025

What I Need You To Know

A Young Girl's Journal on Being Homeless

Written and illustrated by

Elizabeth A. Terrell

Momma's Peanut Butter Cake
Preheat Oven to 325 F

Ingredients
1 stick of unsalted butter
½ c water
½ c smooth peanut butter
½ c vegetable or canola oil
1 tsp. vanilla
2 c sugar
2 c all-purpose flour
1 c sour milk
2 eggs

1 tsp. baking soda
½ tsp. salt

Icing
1 stick butter
⅓ c milk
½ c peanut butter
½ tsp. vanilla
1 16 oz. box confectioners sugar

Put the butter, ½ c peanut butter and the vegetable oil in a saucepan. Bring to a boil as you stir, to keep it from burning. Make sure all of the butter is melted. Pour into a mixing bowl.
Add the vanilla, sugar, flour, milk, eggs, baking soda and salt. Mix well until all is smooth and there are no lumps.
Pour into a greased and floured 9×13 inch baking pan.
Bake for 25 minutes. Cake should pull away from the sides of the pan.
A toothpick inserted in the center should come out clean.

Icing
Put the butter, milk and ½ c peanut butter in a saucepan. Bring to a boil as you stir it. Make sure all of the butter is melted. Remove from the heat. Add the vanilla and confectioners sugar. Mix well until it is smooth. Allow the cake to cool before icing.

This recipe can be altered by using a white cake mix in place of the 2 cups of flour, you then eliminate the baking soda and salt. It will still fit in a 9×13 inch pan but will require about an hour to cook.

1

What I Need You to Know

My name is not important. It could be Maria or Addison, Lakeisha or Neeradj, Soo Li or Morning Sun. It could be Robert or Sean, Malik or Anthony, Carlos or Mikhail. The color of my skin does not matter. My age is of no consequence.

What matters is that I am ~~not~~ Real. I am not made up. I Exist. If only for a short time.

What matters is that you listen.

I have a family; I have a Mother and a little brother. I don't know where my Father is. He left us and if he comes back; I don't know how he'll find us. He knew we were losing the house. He lost his job. The lights got cut off. It was dark. My little brother cried all the time. We had to move.

I had to change schools. I didn't have the right notebooks or paper. I had lost my backpack. My uniforms were the wrong color. At First, I hated everybody, especially me. But it is not so bad in some ways. The roof doesn't leak. It is warm in the winter and the air conditioning feels good on hot days. One of my teachers helped me get some more uniforms. I think she knows how things are, but she doesn't ask me about it. She says she will listen if I need to tell her anything. I cannot tell anyone how it really is. I still hate me.

We used to live with my Momma's friends, sometimes my cousins. But no one really had room for us. We were always in the way. My Mom is working; but there is not enough money for us to stay somewhere. She has almost paid off the old utility bill.

We still get groceries. Momma has found someone who lets us keep our groceries at their house; Momma cooks for everyone after she gets off work. She works at a hamburger place. Sometimes she brings hamburgers for dinner, but the food is counted, even the food that gets thrown away. I try not to think about all the food that gets thrown away. Momma cooks all day and then cooks at night, too. After dinner, Momma and I wash all of the dishes and put them away. We take our baths and then we have to get our things and go. We always have to go. I hate it most when it is raining.

We go out in the rain. Cold rain, hard rain, rain mixed with snow. Humid, hot, summer rain. We go out in the rain. We walk. We come to

3

our hidden space, our secret place that no one else can know about as
we sleep.

Our space is much better than some families have. I know one of my
friends from the church where we eat dinner once a week, sleeps in the
woods in the park with her mother. I have a big refrigerator box that
I sleep in. I have to share it with my little brother. We sleep in an old
garden shed. There are windows on three of the walls. Momma locks us
in every night, then locks the door in the morning. The box makes it
warmer in the winter, but sometimes my brother has a leaky diaper.
I cannot go to school smelling like baby pee. I try not to get mad about it.
Sometimes, I try not to think or feel at all about what we are going through.
I still see beauty in the snowflakes, but I hate being cold. There is no
bathroom. Momma keeps a five gallon bucket with a lid and puts kitty
litter in the bottom just in case we can't wait until morning at the gas
station. Gross. Some nights the stars seem to shine especially bright
as though they shine right through me and I am nothingness. That part
is right. A lot of the time, I am nothingness.

How can one baby hold so much liquid? Does he just save it up for
nighttime? I don't see how people made it before disposable diapers.
No wonder you had to air the mattresses out in the springtime. One
or two babies and the mattress would be toxic.

I get a bicycle today after school. Someone had just put it out;
it only has a flat tire. I'm hoping Momma lets me keep it. She says
we have to be careful about what's in the shed, that it has to look like
storage, not like we live there.

Momma is all excited when she sees me. She doesn't even notice the
bicycle at first. Then she says the bicycle will be fine, she said we'd
ever find a place for it in the shed. She met someone who came into the
restaurant. Momma says they are going to help us get a place to live.
I cannot believe this. It is too much, too much to hope for. Momma
does not say anything to our cousins at dinner and I do not ask.
They can be such dopes. They asked her if she'd met a man. Yeah, like
who would want us! And I already have a father, thank you! I
know his name and what he looks like. But my brother doesn't.
Momma tried to laugh it off but I saw the hurt in her eyes. She never
says anything against my father. We don't really talk about him. It
is hard to remember him and not think about how things used to be. I
can't think about how things used to be. Not now.

Tonight is not so cold. It would be what you would call pleasant if you were walking your dog after dinner and were going home to a comfortable chair and your books or the newspaper. But not to a box. There is a big water bug in the shed. Momma screams. It is my job to get rid of the bugs. I shoo him out the door and we both laugh. Then Momma and I clear out the box and check every inch of the covers to look for more bugs. There are none. Momma talks to me about the woman who is going to help us. Momma wants me to meet her, but now I am not so sure. What if she just wants to take me away? There is a man down the street from my cousin's house. He tried to get me to come eat pizza with him and watch a movie but I don't know him and he doesn't have any kids or a wife or even a girlfriend. Momma says he is up to no good and I am not ever to even walk by his house. What if this woman is not good either? I am too tired to think anymore. Momma makes sure the door is locked and my bicycle is secure against the wall. We don't want any loud noises in the night.

There is a field trip coming up at school, end of the year. I want to go but I know we don't have the money. Momma is trying to save so we can get our own place. Some of the other kids don't think they'll have the money either. If we don't have the money I don't want to go to school that day. I know Momma can't come to the awards program on the last day.

One of the worst things about not having our own place, is trying to do homework. Momma pays to have someone watch my little brother during the day so she can work, but if I get there right after school, they expect me to look after him. Some days, I am so tired; I would love a nap. In the winter, when it gets dark early, I don't like walking by myself from the library. But it is the only place I can really study. There are too many people (including us!) and too much noise and some of them smoke in the house. Don't they read about second hand smoke? I don't want to die because of them, even if my life is nothingness.

Today was really bad. The baby was cranky and they handed him to me right away. I needed to study for my history test. He cried no matter what I did. Finally, I put him in the stroller, got my cards and walked with him. I think he just wanted out of there. I went through my study guide until I knew all of the answers. ~~Them~~ Then we went back to the house. They were mad and wanted me to start dinner because Momma was going to be late. I did. But it wasn't fair. They were there and I had the baby. Why couldn't they start dinner? I was really glad when Momma got there.

After dinner, as we walked to our secret place, I told her about my day. I told her about the field trip money and my history test and my little brother and having to start dinner. She listened to everything. She says she will get the money for the field trip. She is proud of me for studying and for looking after my brother, especially at the same time. She said she knew it was hard not to say anything but to just start dinner. It is hard for her at work sometimes not to say anything back when someone complains. I love my Momma and the time we have together.

Momma has talked with the woman again. She gave Momma a tape measure to measure the windows so she can get screens for the windows and some burglar bars; we could open the windows if we needed to and still be safe. I am tired and my little brother is already asleep. We do a quick check for bugs and then go to sleep. I fall asleep reviewing my history questions in my head. Momma is going to meet with the worker tomorrow. I sure hope this lady is OK.

I think I did OK, "did well" as my English teacher would say, on my history test. Finding some quiet time helped. School will be out in a month. I will die if things don't change by the time school starts back. Even before then. The summer will be Hades at the cousins house. There is going to have to be somewhere else for me to go.

Tonight, Momma and I measure the windows, top to bottom and side to side, all of them. The worker wants the screens to go all the way over the windows. She says they are probably double hung. I dropped the pen and Momma and I made an amazing discovery, both wonderful and scary. Behind the box of old hymnals and children's Sunday School books, is ... an electrical outlet. We looked at it in disbelief. How could it be there and us not know? If it works we could have a light or a heater or a fan... Momma says we can't try it out. We will have to wait and be very careful. If we used it, someone might see the light and know we were there. Someone might figure out we were using the electricity and come looking for the source. We don't want to cheat anyone or be accused of stealing electricity. We sure don't want anyone to know that we are here. Even God has to keep our secret. Momma will bring a small lamp from our storage stuff and we will see if it works tomorrow.

I am so excited. I know other people would not understand but it would be so wonderful to have a light. Now Momma is really concerned about who owns the shed. Our shed is actually at the back of a church, except the church is on the next lot and there is a fence, a lacy looking wire fence, between us. Maybe there is a gate in the overgrown hedge. Maybe that's why there are old hymnals and Sunday School books in the box. Maybe Momma can get the worker to find out who owns the shed.

Momma talked to the worker. If we can get the address of the church, she will find out if they own the lot our shed is on. If we give her the address of the church, she will know where we are at night. What if she turns us in? This is so scary. It just makes my stomach tie in knots and hurt.

I can hardly wait until we finish dinner and get the dishes done. Momma went by the storage place and now there is a small lamp tucked into the baby carriage. I wanted to run to the shed. It is warmer now and Momma has folded our box flat. We put our blankets on top with the baby between us. There is also a layer of plastic and newspapers under him in case his diaper leaks. He is asleep by the time we get there. We walk a little further, first around the back block, to check the address of the church. Then we go home. We use our flashlights. I wait impatiently while my Mother puts my little brother to bed, saying silent prayers as he stays asleep while Momma moves him. We say our prayers together and Momma gets the lamp. It is a small brass lamp from my room, my stuff. Just for an instant, my mind flashes back to my room... mustn't go there, cannot go there, cannot think about that now. Momma finds the outlet and clears away the dust. She plugs it in. The room is illuminated. Just as quickly, she turns the light out. The safety of darkness. She presses another carefully wrapped package into my hands. ~~My~~ I begin to unwrap it. My hands run over the smooth, shiny plastic and metal casing. Even in the darkness, I know what it is. The tears start to flow and I cannot stop them. Momma holds me and I cry and I cry and I cry. My brother continues to sleep. I hold the radio, my old red heart shaped clock radio from the antique shop on the corner. Where Momma and I used to go, in my old life. I, too, am old now.

It takes several ~~days for~~ for our worker to look up the property address and get back to us. The church behind us does own the property. And not only is there electricity, but there are water lines and gas lines. At one time, there was an old two story house with a big front porch on the property. Now what do we do?

Momma has the screens for the windows. We can have air, a breeze blowing through. It is not easy, putting up window screens with a flashlight, trying to be quiet and laughing at how ridiculous it is. They didn't seem to fit at first but the windows were not all the same size, so we had to try them until they fit. We will only be able to open them at night. The next thing will be bars for the windows. I wish I could take the flashlight and go look for the water spigot, but Momma says it will be too risky.

Momma surprises me with interesting news. The church behind us is going to have a bake sale. Momma is going to make 2 pies and a cake. She will donate one of the pies but sell the other one and the cake. She will have to get off work early on Friday for the sale on Saturday. This will be my field trip money for next Friday. I am going to help.

Momma makes dinner early and I do the dishes while she gets everything ready. Clean hands, clean counters, all the ingredients, and extra people out of the kitchen. The cousins have gone to Friday Night Wrestling at the colisum downtown. Finally we are ready. There will be apple pie, peach cobbler and peanut butter cake. We will carry them home in the wagon. I get to help measure ingredients, roll out the dough, run the mixer and ice the cake. It takes a long time. We are exhausted when we finish. Momma has brought two smaller boxes for the pie and the cake and a flat box for the cobbler. The cousins come back late, after 10 o'clock and we start for home. I wish someone could push me in a stroller and I could sleep on the way home. Everything smells so good. Momma is the best cook, but I still want to be a veterinarian.

Not only did we get home late, we had to get up early. We had to take my baby brother to the sitter's for the morning, but we had to make sure no one saw us leave our shed. We would've spent the night at the cousin's house but Momma and I were afraid they would eat the pie, the cobbler and the cake. I wanted to eat them myself. Why not have peach cobbler for breakfast? Momma lets me have coffee with her. I put a little more milk in mine, but it always tastes better out of her cup. Momma says it is the love in it that makes it taste better.

We eat breakfast at the sitter's house and then take our wagon of baked treasures to the church. I hope they know how to make good coffee.

It is an old, grey stone church. I have always thought that it was beautiful. The bake sale is in the basement or the first floor, depending on where you come in. Momma puts the apple pie on the donation table. It looks so good. A woman comes and gives us name tags to wear. I find the coffee before Momma does and point it out to her. We head that way first. We get our coffee.

make our way to our table. We can sell our cobbler whole or price it by the dish. It is so pretty with its browned crust, the peach filling peeking out and the light reflecting off the sugar crystals. It smells heavenly. Momma decides to sell the cobbler whole. We will cut the cake into slices. Momma cuts the cake into 36 pieces; it is what is known as a sheet cake. We sip our coffee and talk with the other people around us. No one else brought cobbler or a peanut butter cake. There are several chocolate cakes. There is one cheesecake. If I had the money and we had a refrigerator, I would buy the cheesecake. Momma and I could eat it every night after dinner until all of it was gone.

A man stops by to look at our cobbler. He asks about the cake. I tell him that Momma is the best cook and that the cake goes really good with coffee. He buys a piece. He eats it. He buys another piece, takes a bite and says, "I'll be back." He brings a woman back with him. The woman looks at me. My heart is racing. Oh, no, what is wrong? Then she says, "doesn't your Momma work at the hamburger place?" Thank God that is all that it is. I find my words. "Yes, she does. But her talents are really not best used there," I reply. "Oh, I can tell that, honey. We want to buy the whole cake. We also would like to talk to her about a job at our restaurant. In fact, here's $50 and we'll just take the cobbler, too. Is that enough?"

I find my voice and my manners. "Yes, ma'am, that's more than enough. This means I can go on the school field trip." Thankfully, Momma comes back and introduces herself. I just sit there and smile, holding tight to our $50. The coffee tastes so good. It has been a long time since I held $50. I think of all the things that $50 will buy, depending on where you spend it. When gas is high, it would buy a tank for the car or the pickup truck. It could buy almost half the utility deposit, one ticket for the ballet in the higher up section, a tune up and a tire for my bicycle, new shoes on sale, a pet from the animal shelter, lots of dark chocolate and good coffee. Momma is still talking to the people so I point to my cup and the coffee area. I take her cup, too. I get Momma some more coffee, being careful not to spill it as I walk. Even after the coffee, I could still nap. I take a sip of Momma's coffee before I hand it to her. It is always better from her cup. There is love in it. She smiles, and says, "thank you, ~~sweet~~ sweetheart," as I hand it to her. When I was little, Momma called me "Precious" so often that someone thought it was my name. She still calls me Precious.

Finally, finally, finally, they finish talking. That man ate at least one other piece of cake while they talked. His wife looks as though she is going to guard the cobbler and make him wait until dinnertime to eat more. Momma would do that, too.

We leave with our empty wagon to go get my brother. I am so excited. We have field trip money and Momma has an extra $30 and I helped earn it! Momma has a new job, maybe. She says she has to think about it and work things out. What is there to work out? It's not like her job now cares about her or us. When I got sick last year, I would've had to walk to my cousin's house because the hamburger place would not let Momma off. One of the teacher's aides took me home. We stayed at the cousins' house for several days until I was well enough to walk home at night. Momma cried for 2 nights straight and wouldn't talk to me about it. Momma says the professional thing to do is to give two weeks notice.

Tonight we are going to eat dinner at the new restaurant. All of us, but not my cousins. I still don't think we're related—we don't like any of the same things.

We pick up my brother and head for the cousins' house to do laundry. They are upset that Momma will not be fixing dinner for everyone. I can see it in Momma's face that she is thinking of everything else while we do laundry and I play with my brother. How many times can we do peek-a-boo? Momma is writing her resignation letter and figuring up the bills. Deciding about childcare and what she should wear

11

tonight and somewhere I hope she still wonders where my Daddy is. I do. My brother is sleepy and so am I. Momma finds us a clean, quiet, comfy place to nap. Nonsmoking of course. Not an easy task in this house. I think we're actually sleeping in what may have been the back porch at one time. There are exposed bricks and lots of windows, the ceiling is tongue and groove and there is the wonderful ceiling fan. And the smell of our clean, folded laundry. My brother falls asleep first and I fall asleep listening to the ceiling fan and his rhythmic, peaceful baby breaths.

Momma takes him when he begins to stir and I drift back to sleep for a little while longer. Blissful, safe, and hopeful sleep. Not worried about bugs, or someone finding us, someone harming us. Tonight could change our lives. I could have a bed again, my own bed, my own space.

Momma is ready when I finally wake up and knows what my little brother is going to wear. His bag is packed and waiting. I take a shower and let the hot water pound the tensions in my back. Momma says I do not have to dress up. I pick out my best jeans and my favorite earrings. We will come back here before we go home. I think about who may be at the restaurant and what questions they make may ask. I know all the safe answers. We are going to need to hide for a little while longer, even if Momma takes this job. So far, the owners seem really nice and the man really loves Momma's desserts.

It is time to go. The cousins actually give us a ride to the restaurant. They are even going to pick us up. Usually, they charge us money but they want Momma to make them a peach cobbler this weekend, just for them.

The restaurant is a family style place and there are lots of children. Children with mommas and daddys and children with just mommas. Even children with grandparents. All ages and races of people. The tables are round and seat 6 to 8 people. There are smaller tables mixed in that seat 4 people with some booths along the wall by the windows. There is real silverware, not plastic, and plates that probably break if you drop them. There is a buffet and a menu. There is so much food. I want to know what they do with the leftovers and how much food do they waste and throw out. I know I can't ask tonight, I will have to wait. But I will ask. Momma is looking at everything. The owners come to welcome us. Evidently, everyone who got to taste the cobbler and the peanut butter cake, loved it. They are both all gone. We get a highchair for my brother and decide what to eat. Momma and I both decide to eat from the buffet. I have ham and potato salad and green beans, a buttery biscuit, sweet potatoes and some kind of baked squash. Momma tries the roast, fried okra, turnip greens, sweet corn and cornbread. My brother gets sweet potatoes and green beans. Momma and I have cheesecake for dessert. It is all so good. Then we have coffee. I wait with my brother while Momma tours the kitchen. Momma will talk with them on Sunday after church. She calls the cousins and we wait outside for them to pick us up. Momma will have to make their cobbler tomorrow.

There will be a lot for us to talk about as we walk home tonight. Momma and I will try to sleep a little later tomorrow.

At the cousins' house, Momma and I quickly gather our things for the walk home. Momma promises to have the peach cobbler ready for them by dinnertime on Sunday.

Momma is excited about working at the restaurant. She liked the size of it, where it is, that lots of different people come, that it is family oriented, that she will have Sunday off. For now, she will only be responsible for making desserts. She will have a certain area of the kitchen and a certain oven to use. She will go to work after I go to school and be off at 3PM. I cannot believe it. We can spend time together in the afternoons and I will be able to get my homework done and not be a junior momma. She does not know how often I have ended up with my brother lately and I will not tell her. She is going to take the job. She will give her notice on Monday.

We check to make sure that no one is around and make our way to the door in the darkness. Once again we are safe inside our door. Hidden, unknown, anonymous.

We turn on our flashlights as Momma locks us in. She hands me a small package, wrapped in a brown paper sack and then rolled in tissue paper. It is not my birthday or anything like that I can think of. "Open it," she says. "It is because I love you and you are my daughter." I love you gifts are always special. Carefully, but quickly I unwrap the rolls of tissue paper. It is a pink crystal angel night-light. Her wings are open and her arms are raised, to welcome and protect, and ... she has curly hair. There is a switch to turn the light on and off. It will give us a little light at night but not attract attention from the outside. She is beautiful. I plug her in and we both are struck by the transformation of our little space by the faceted crystal light. We check for bugs, put my brother between us and lay down. One last look at the patterns of light and I cut off the light. I kiss Momma and my brother goodnight. We say our I love you's and fall asleep. We are exhausted.

Saturday and Sunday mornings are hard because we have to stay hidden but still get out of the house "in broad daylight" as Momma would say. Which always makes me wonder—what does narrow daylight look like? Maybe that kind of daylight is for us—the people of nothingness. People who are looked down on. It is early still and it is always easier to leave when it is early. Church behind us is nowhere near ready to start or have somebody in the parking lot. We dress quickly and quietly, making sure we have all of my brother's things. My brother and I leave first, looking as though I am his big sister taking him for a walk. Momma makes sure the door is locked and comes a few minutes later. I sometimes see young mothers pushing their babies and also walking the dog. I can see myself with a dog, a medium to a large dog to protect us, but gentle and faithful or maybe a happy, little cocker spaniel who would play fetch with me in the afternoons and on weekends. She could sleep on my bed and cuddle with me at night. She could ~~sleep on my bed~~ listen to all of my secrets. She could... my mind and my heart race on. If we didn't live in a garden shed.

Momma puts her hand on mine, "Things are getting better, Precious. We are going to have a place to live." I smile back at her. It has been hard for her, too. I want to ask about Daddy, but I cannot bring myself to form the words. For now, it has to be enough that we have made it through the night, that I have field trip money and Momma has another job. Maybe it will be different, maybe when they count the food it won't have to be thrown away and we won't have to go hungry. Maybe there will be enough money.

We stop at the gas station, buy a Sunday paper and use the restroom. Then we head for breakfast at a fast food restaurant - our treat. After breakfast, we walk back to the church behind our garden shed house, actually their garden shed, and slip quietly into the back row of the chapel for the early service. I love to listen to the pipe organ. I confess that I don't always listen to the sermon. Momma usually knows all the hymns and loves to sing them; she can hit all of the really high notes. I know the hymns from listening to her and now, from the old hymn books in our shed. Today, I even have money for the offering. They are baptizing a baby today and as we sing a special hymn that I love, the pastor walks up and down the aisles carrying the baby. We have a baby; I don't remember him being baptized. I look at Momma, it is as though she is reading my mind. Then she is crying and we leave. I wonder if it is a special wrong thing to make your Mother cry in church on a Sunday. Momma cries for the next two blocks, doesn't say anything, just cries. On the third block, she stops crying because we are getting close to the restaurant and she can't be crying. I want to cry, too.

15

But if I start crying, my brother will cry, too. Can't have feelings right now, can't have feelings.

The restaurant is not open, but we knock on the door and someone, smiling, lets us in. I sit down at a table to wait for Momma as she heads back to the kitchen. We still have a cobbler to make for this afternoon. Tomorrow, I can turn in my field trip money. Why didn't Momma and Daddy have my brother baptized? I know they did me. Momma showed me pictures before, taken at another church and at our home and ... I can't go there. Not in my mind, not in reality. The tables look as though they are set for dinner at someone's home, a Sunday dinner. We have a table, somewhere, in storage. Too bad you can't put houses in storage.

Momma comes back. Everything is settled. She will start work here next Monday, but she will still be able to give 2 weeks notice at her other job by using her vacation week. I had hoped we could use her vacation week as a vacation. Not go anywhere but just have her to be off. Momma gets coffee to go and I get lemonade. We go to the park. I love to swing. Momma says that when I was little like my brother, she put me in a backpack and took me swinging. The backpack may be in storage.

When I am swinging, I like to go as high as I can. Hold tight to the chains and point my feet into the sky. Sometimes I close my eyes and just feel the wind in my face. Today, I swing for a long time. I make myself stop because we still have to walk to the cousins' house and cook and make cobbler.

The cousins are mad, really mad. They are yelling at each other about who is supposed to pay the utility bill. I know it is not us. But we will have one in the future. In the future ... such strange words. Even a few days ago, I wondered if we had a future, now we do. I'm glad my Mother doesn't yell. It will be nice to have our own utility bill, our own place, our own space.

Momma makes everybody get out of the kitchen. We clean

the countertops and the stove. Now we are ready. Momma makes the dough while I wash, peel and cut up peaches. There is the wonderful smell of dough and cinnamon and peaches. Cooking is such a loving kind of smell. I know you don't have to love someone to cook for them but home cooking has to have love int in it. I know Momma's does and she loves to cook. I forget about the cousins and eventually they are quiet, or as quiet as they can ever be. I still don't see how we are related to them. They must be "play" cousins like some of my friends at school have or cousins "once removed" (whatever that means) who were mistakenly "put back" with our family. It is OK. They don't think that we fit with them either.

We wait for the cobbler to get done. We clean up all of our baking dishes. I go get our things ready. Momma makes salads for everybody and chicken salad sandwiches with wonderful tomato slices and the good kind of lettuce. There was leftover dough and peaches, so Momma made a tiny cobbler just for us. She even used one of our pans so nobody can say anything. I think cooking should be an act of peacemaking, not smoking a pipe. The cobblers come out of the oven. Momma sets them on the stove. She wraps ours in foil and newspapers and puts it in a sack. I will carry it home. The other one will not last long. We gather our things up and get my brother. I make sure that I have my field trip money for tomorrow. It may rain tonight but we will be safe. Our garden shed house roof does not leak. We step out into the night, the scent of the cobbler marking our trail.

Momma and I sit in the floor, eating cobbler and talking in whispers. We laugh, thinking about the cousins and no one paying the utility bill. It feels good to laugh. But the reality is, if they don't pay it we won't be able to have groceries and to cook there. Momma realizes that, too. We say a special prayer of thanksgiving for them that we can cook there and then we go to bed.

The rain comes and comes and comes. But our little garden shed home withstands the wind and the rain. Fortunately, it stops before we have to leave in the morning. It is sprinkling, but it is not coming down in torrents. It was so loud last night, I stood at the window and watched, as sheets of rain came down in waves. I thought about my friend who sometimes still has to sleep outside with her Mother and I said a special prayer for her.

My brother laughs and tries to catch the drops of rain as we walk. Momma will turn in her notice today at work and I will turn in my cobbler/cake field trip money. I have $10 extra saved, too. Sometimes we have to have extra money for lunch.

I can tell that my teacher is relieved that I have my money. It's as though she wants us all to be able to go, as much as we want to go. My friend is crying softly, behind me. Her Mother signed her paper but she doesn't have all of her money. She has half of it, but she needs $10 more. If I give up my extra $10, she will have enough. It is my money, I do not think my Mother would mind. I tell my teacher when she calls me up to take the attendance card to the office. Attendance has to be on the computer and on paper at the end of the year. She says she will take care of it, that she knows someone who will help. She lets my friend go with me to the office so I can tell her that she is going on the trip, too. It is not supposed to rain on Friday. I will use my $10 with my friend at lunch on Friday. I can hardly believe we are both getting to go.

The day passes quickly. I want to know how Momma's day went. My friend is as excited as I am. Our trip will be a great way to start the summer. I hope Momma can find somewhere else for us to go other than the cousins' house. Otherwise, I will have my brother to watch and be at the mercy of the cousins. Momma does not know how bad that can actually be.

I stop by the library on the way to the cousins' house. They have some new books. When we get a real address, I can have a library card. Then I can check out books and movies and everything. I use the computer to look up some information on things we have been studying. It would be wonderful to have a computer or a laptop at home. To have a home again. It seems so long ago. Sometimes I wonder if I imagined my whole life before and only the life I have now is real. Sometimes I panic when I think about it, what if this is not temporary, what if someone finds out where we are, what if my Daddy never comes back... I have to stop. My time at the computer is over and I have to go. It is warm outside, but not too hot. The sun is hidden behind the clouds of last night's rain. I watch for worms on the sidewalk and put them back in the grass. There are still some puddles left and I would like to walk barefoot in them but I know I can't now. Momma would let me, she would not care; I could take my little brother, too. There will be other rains, and other puddles that I will get to walk through.

At the cousins' house, no one has brought in the mail yet. It is a little damp and hard to get out of the box. There is an odd letter, a brown envelope, from the army, with Momma's name on it. Daddy was in the army, before I was born. Why would they send Momma a letter? I take the letter from the pile and quickly stuff it into my backpack. I knock on the door and someone lets me in. I put the mail on the table and go check on my brother. He is sleeping. I am hungry. I find the plastic storage bin in the back room where he is and quietly open it. This is where my afterschool snacks are supposed to be. There are hardly any snacks left. Someone has taken them. I eat dried fruit, peanut butter crackers and a chocolate nutrition drink. This is so unfair. They don't want me in the refrigerator, even for a glass of cold water and yet, they came back here and ate my snacks. I do what little homework I have and take a nap. Momma will be home soon. Tonight she's making hamburgers and french fries. I will make the salads.

I am awakened by loud, angry voices and the crying of my brother. "Where's the mail? Did we get another army letter? Did they send the check?" Instantly, I am awake. Another army letter? A check? I gather up my brother into my arms and hold him close. I sing softly to him. I shake my head at him. Dirty diaper. "This is stinky. You should have waited til Momma get home." He laughs. I change him and carry him with me to the front of the house. But not before I take the army letter, fold it small and stuff it into my jeans pocket.

19

Whatever it is, it is important and Momma has to have it.

I put my brother in the high chair with some dry cereal on his tray. We are in the kitchen so I can start dinner. I begin by washing lettuce, carrots, and tomatoes for the salads. Then lettuce, tomatoes and onions for the burgers. Wash the potatoes, cut out the eyes and discolored spots, slice them for fries. Momma is still not here. Make the meat into patties, all about the same size and thickness. Still no Momma. I start to heat the oil for the french fries. I hear the front door. Momma. I breathe a sigh of relief. She puts her things away and gets a cup of coffee. I get a hug and a kiss and a thank you for starting dinner. I tell her about my day. My brother babbles away as though he, too, has something to tell. I'm sure he does after being here all day. The letter is burning a hole in my pocket but I cannot say anything now. Instead, I let my brother sniff an onion. He wrinkles his nose and turns away.

The fast food restaurant wants Momma to help them find someone to take her place. My friend's mother is trying to find a job and the fast food restaurant would be more regular hours. Momma will talk to her. I will tell my friend tomorrow. The french fries are wonderful. Brown and crisp and hot. One of the cousins ate three burgers and he doesn't even work. How can he eat like that? There was no cobbler left from yesterday. They want to talk to Momma.

I wash the dishes and clean up in the kitchen while Momma talks to them in the living room. If she is going to work at the family restaurant, they want more money, even though we don't stay here at night. They want the money up front, not when she gets paid. Momma doesn't make that much. What are we going to do? They must want us to pay the utility bill.

I help Momma pack up our things. I take enough snacks for tomorrow afternoon. Momma makes sure we have everything and we say goodnight.

Momma has a surprise. Someone put out a small, old oscillating fan and it works. Momma has already tried it out. It will give us a nice breeze tonight. Momma says she will put extra money in the offering at church to cover the electricity. It is a risk though. Someone could figure out that we are there.

I let Momma talk. I let her tell me about how hard it is in some ways to leave her job at the fast food restaurant because she cares about the people she works with, especially the ones she supervises. But she knows it is time to go. I ask her about what the cousins want, and she tells me not to worry about it. She says we will manage. She says the HOW is trying to find us a place to live. I had almost forgotten about her; Momma says the worker is excited about Momma's new job. That the worker is trying to find a camp for me to go to in the day for the summer and a place for my brother. The worker wants to know what kinds of things I want to do and what I like to do.

I want to go skating and to ride my bike. I want to swim until I am exhausted. I want to walk in the puddles that the rain left. I want to have a dog and a cat or two. Wait, that last one really has to wait. A dog and 2 cats have nothing to do with summer camp. A horse camp or a camp where I work with animals would be good. A chance to do more art would be good. Knowing how to fix basic things on a computer would be good. I share all this with Momma except about the dog and the 2 cats. Momma laughs and says she doesn't know if one camp can do all of these things, but that they will try to find one that I like.

We are at the gas station. Momma and I go to the restrooms one more time. Outside, the letter is about to explode in my pocket and I can wait no longer. I ask Momma to wait there in the light because I have something important to tell her, for her to read. I start to tell her the whole story, but I can't. I am scared. What if my Daddy is dead and the army somehow knows? I almost cannot talk. Momma is worried and anxious and concerned. Finally, I blurt it all out like dropping groceries on the sidewalk when the sack breaks. "This letter came today. I brought in the mail. The cousins don't know I took it. It is for you, not them."

21

Momma hugs me, says everything will be ok no matter what is in the letter. She opens the letter and quickly scans it, then she starts to cry. I can't bear it. I sit down on the sidewalk. Numb, the deadness rising inside of me. Momma wraps her arms around me. "Precious, Precious, your Daddy is alright. We are alright. We are going to be fine." Then she explains. When Daddy left, he left to find a job. When he couldn't find a regular job, he re-enlisted in the army. We had already left the house and he couldn't find us. All this time, he has been looking for us. The army wrote Momma a letter and sent it to the cousins' house, trying to find us. Momma says Daddy wants to send us part of his paycheck. (I didn't know they paid people to be in the army.) Now Momma has to prove who we are, related to Daddy, by sending them different papers. She will have to go to the storage place and get the papers. Then they have to be notarized and sent back to the person and address in the letter. Then they will send the check. Actually, they want to send it direct deposit.

Momma is telling me all of this and all I can think about is Daddy. Now we have to find a place to live. We can't be living in a garden shed, even though it's a nice garden shed behind a church, when Daddy comes back.

Momma goes back in the gas station and buys a big candy bar. We split it and eat chocolate as we walk home.

The fan works great. I go to sleep with a cooling breeze and a million questions in my mind. I am so glad that Momma knows what to do. I say a special thank you prayer for Daddy.

Momma will go to the storage place today and find our papers. She will get everything notarized and mailed on Wednesday. She makes sure I have her work phone number to give to my friend to give to to her Momma. Momma says I won't be able to write Daddy or talk to him or email him until we send in our papers and prove who we are. How can I even think about school today? How can it only be Tuesday?

At school, I find my friend first and give her the phone number. I try to tell her the people are not nice and that her Mother may have to work extra hours, but they will pay her for all of her hours. She says her Mother does not care. They will have groceries and rent money and utilities. Her Mother has already found an apartment. It has a playground and a swimming pool. She says a lady is helping them. The woman is going to help them with the deposit and the first month's rent. This woman sounds like our HOW. I do not say anything, I just listen. I do not know where my friend lives right now and I do not ask. I only know it is not a place I can visit. She knows she cannot visit me either. We both want to visit, to have sleepovers and stay up late and eat pizza. It is hard to be homeless and to be quiet about it, always guarding a big secret. A secret you can't let out. My friend knows. We both have to be quiet a little longer. The bell rings and we walk to the classroom.

Today we are studying some subjects that we will study next year. We will have a different teacher for this subject next year but at least this interesting. We are going to pack our books up on Thursday; I have already brought all of mine in. Tomorrow we are going to have a field day. Late this afternoon we are going to get all of the equipment ready. I think I am the fastest runner and my friend jumps double dutch jump rope better than anyone I have ever seen. We take our last spelling test and math test. Tomorrow we will take our last reading test. I am so looking forward to having a real address and getting a library card. Then I can have books to read whenever I want. I'll have to keep them hidden from my little brother though, he likes to shred paper. It has been hard this year to keep my books from getting damaged. I finally lined my bookbag with a large, plastic bag. That way, I could still carry my books in my bookbag in the rain.

At lunch, we have hamburgers, of all things. I am hungry. They are nowhere near as good as Mother's but it is what we have and I eat it. My friend and I switch desserts. We both drink our milk.

After lunch we have art class. Usually we don't get to have art for an hour but today we do. We are doing paper weavings. The teacher explains what we are going to do. We have to choose a background color and then weave strips of paper in and out. I choose a

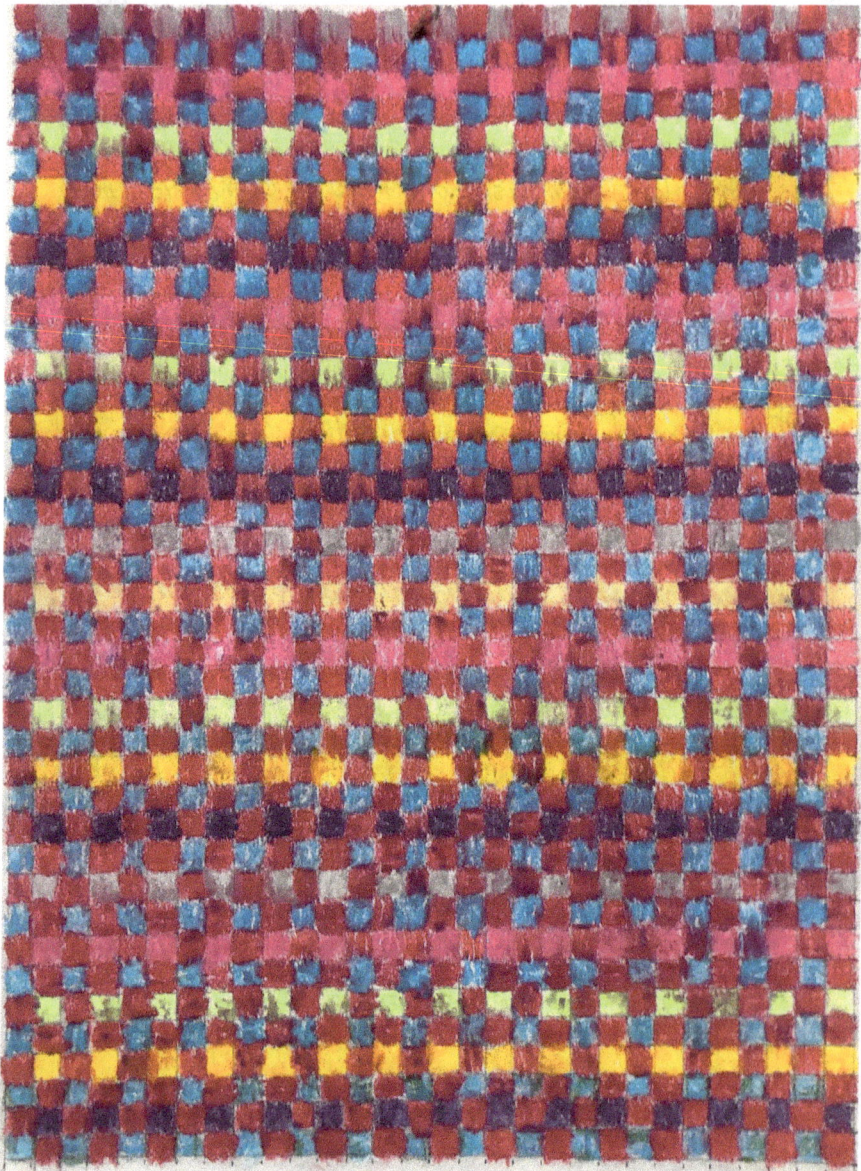

bright pink for the background. Then I will use light pink, green, blue, purple and yellow, with a pale orange one in the middle. Some of the students try to rush through but you have to pay attention to the pattern to make it look right. It takes most of the hour. When they are finished, we write our name on the back and place them along the board rail. They are beautiful. So many different color combinations all woven in the same pattern. Like us, all the strips of paper are needed and all belong.

We divide into teams and get out the equipment we will need for field day. Gloves, bases, bats, balls, ropes, hula hoops, stop watches. We can bring our own skates.

We have worked hard today. As a surprise, our teacher lets us choose a soft drink and choose a game to play for the last 45 minutes of the day. My friend and choose Scrabble. We try to see who can come up with the silliest words that will make us laugh. It feels good to sit and laugh.

My friend and I walk part way home together, then she goes down one block and I go down the other to the cousins' house. I knock on the door and wait. Once in, I am thankful to be in the back porch room. I still have time for a nap. I eat my snacks quietly and think about tomorrow. We can wear regular clothes and bring extra snacks. I know I still have clean clothes. Momma took the rest of my snacks. I want to look at pictures of Daddy and open the boxes in storage and smell the cologne scent on his shirts. I want him back. I go to sleep thinking about Daddy and being a family again.

There is loud talking, not quite yelling - the cousins. I hear Momma's soft voice, tired and patient. They want more money. They want to know where I will be this summer and who will watch after my brother. The HOW woman has found me a summer camp. A bus will come pick me up and bring me home. She said a church is paying for it. Wouldn't it be funny if it is the same church that owns our garden shed house?

Momma comes and gives me a hug, says that she loves me. She has the papers to prove who we are. We talk about my day, about the paper weavings and about field day. We laugh about eating hamburgers.

Momma has a dinner surprise. She went by the restaurant and picked up chicken salad- not the kind with mayonnaise but grilled chicken we can have over a green salad. There is green Romaine lettuce and spinach leaves, carrots to cut, bell peppers in 3 colors, sweet onion bits, shredded cheese and boiled eggs, tomatoes, wonderful red tomatoes. We also have dark red kidney beans, corn and baked apples. I like to put the kidney beans and corn in with my salad. The colors and textures are beautiful when we are done. There are no leftovers to be put away tonight. Momma has one last cup of coffee as we do the dishes. I am ready to go to bed. My brother is already having trouble staying awake.

Momma got my skates out of storage. I had forgotten that I had them. I think they will still fit. She got the papers and got them notarized. Notarized means she proved to someone who we are and they signed their name under Momma's name, dated it and put this big embossed seal on it. Momma opened a bank account today, too. She's using a post office box as our address. It may be two weeks before we know anything.

It is warm outside. The smell of flowers hangs in the air like a welcoming to come home. Home, a real home, a place beyond our garden shed. A room of my own with a window to look into the backyard, our backyard. A fenced safe backyard where we could play and cook out and have friends over and the dog could play. At night the dog(s) could sleep in my room. I want my old metal bed-frame back, the one Momma slept in as a child with her sister. There will be bookshelves for all of my books and space for new ones. I can see it all. My mind is full, my heart is full and Momma is quiet, too. My brother is already asleep and we are almost home. We stop at the gas station and fill our water jugs. Everything we do now has a different meaning, a different way to look at it. We will not have to do this forever. There will be an end, a change, a new beginning. We will be like the butterflies emerging from the cocoons.

Momma has already sent off the papers, they went in today's mail. They had to go by regular mail. We are on our street. We always have to make sure that no one is watching and that no one is following

26

us, we have to be safe. Momma looks around and I do, too. There is a noise, it sounds like crying - a baby or a small animal. I hope it is a kitten or a puppy. We look around again. No one is there. No one but the noise.

Momma turns on the flashlight and begins to sweep it from side to side along the path in front of us, as we move quietly toward the shed and the noise. A puppy or a kitten would be so wonderful. My baby brother wakes up, alert, he hears the noise. He begins to babble as though talking. The noise comes again and then a different sound. My brother is excited, kicking and babbling, waving his arms. Surely, no one has left a baby here. Momma shines the light in a big sweep across the field, something small and dark moves, then is still. Another cry startles us as we come close to the steps. My brother is trying to get out of the stroller. There beside the steps in a pink baby carrier care seat is a beautiful baby girl. There are small brown muddy prints on her blanket. There is a puppy or a kitten somewhere. My Mother is speechless at first. Then she exclaims, "Someone has left us a baby. A beautiful, precious baby girl - how could they ever think we could take in a baby?" Just then, there is a rustling in the grass. A damp, black ~~curely~~ curly ball of fur comes bounding out of the grass and lands on my feet, its whole body wagging. My brother claps his hands in absolute delight. I scoop up the puppy as Momma reaches for the baby.

The puppy still has puppy breath and baby teeth; it is young. I put it close to my brother. He shifts the pup and buries his face in its curly black fur. The pup licks him in the face. Momma has the baby, talking to her, swatting mosquitoes away from her face and searching for a note, identification, anything. The baby bag has clothes, diapers and formula, wipes, powder and extra bottles. I search the bag as Momma holds the baby and I hold the puppy. Finally, I find a note. It is written on a scrap of paper torn from an old utility bill. It says:

Please take my baby girl. Her name is Emily.
I have watched you for awhile. I know that
you are good Mother. I will leave all of her
papers for you at the new restaurant.
                    Love,
                    Emily's Mother

The puppy's name is Teacup

Momma and I look at each other. I speak first because I
can't wait any longer. "Momma, what are we going to do? It's
kind of creepy that that woman has been watching us. I mean, I'm
glad she thinks we are good people and would take care of her baby,
but I don't know who she is. I'm glad she left us the puppy."

Momma answered "Precious, I know you are happy about the
puppy. It's this baby, Emily, that has my concern." I rubbed my
face against the puppy's soft fur. It made little noises as it went to
sleep in my lap. All of a sudden I had a horrifying thought.

"Momma, if we call the police, they will know where we are and try
to take all of us! We can't keep Emily without someone knowing."
The tears began to flood down my face as the puppy snuggled closer
to me. "Momma, I'll die if I have to go somewhere else." Momma
puts her arms around me and holds me tight. "No one is going to
take you away from me, Sweetheart. No one."

"Tonight, we will all go to bed, even the puppy. In the morning,
you will go to school. I will take your brother to the cousins'
house as usual. I will call our HOW and explain to her what has
happened. I think there is enough ventilation in the shed for
Teacup pup. She will cry at first when we leave but she should be
fine. We will have to clean up after her when we get home. Agreed?"

"Oh, yes, Momma, I will clean up after Teacup. Momma, I'm
sorry we can't keep Emily. She deserves a home, too."

My brother begins to fuss. He knew he wasn't getting any attention.
I put Teacup down and pick up my brother, then scoop up a sleepy puppy.
We bed down Emily and my brother first. Then Momma on one side of
them and me on the other. I snuggle Teacup next to me on the other side.

She sucked my fingers before stretching out and going to sleep.

The morning came before I was ready. I took Teacup out to go to the bathroom. I talked to her about how wonderful she was and how glad I was to have her. She listened and licked my nose when I held her close to my face. I let her run around the shed while I helped Momma change Emily and my brother to get them ready to go. One more baby is so much more to do.

Finally we are ready. I gather my bookbag with my skates and Emily's things, setting them in the stroller. Momma brings my brother and I carry Emily. I stop to kiss Teacup goodbye. I show her where her water is and tell her she has to wait for us. I remind her that I already love her. She cries when I shut the door and lock it, but she quiets down real quick. She is quiet by the time we walk away. Momma says that is good that Teacup will not cry a lot and give away our hiding place.

I cannot believe it. I have a puppy, a pretty, little girl puppy all my own. I feel sorry for Emily. She doesn't have her Mother. It would not be bad to have a Baby sister. I hold her close and stroke her dark, curly hair, like little dark springs on her head. She has that sweet baby smell. She looks at me with her serious brown eyes and puts her head against my chest. We are getting close to my school. I give Emily a kiss and pass her over to my Mother. Mother gives me a hug and a kiss, tells me she loves me and that I am wonderful. I know she will look after everything. I run to find my friend to tell her my news, my skates thumping against my back in my bookbag.

At breakfast, I tell my friend about the puppy. She cannot believe someone left us a baby and a puppy. She does not want anyone to leave her Mother a baby. She does not think they could deal with a puppy right now either. We eat our breakfast - blueberry muffins and milk with a sausage patty and half a peach. I save the seed from my peach. I will have a place to plant it later. We finish our breakfast and talk about field day until the bell rings.

In class, we will be doing at least math and reading. For reading, we are reading a library book in class and writing a paragraph about what we think. Then we will listen to our teacher read to us from a chapter book she has. We have math worksheets. I finish mine and get it checked. Now I can work as a peer tutor with people who are having trouble.

It is almost time. Our teacher talks with us about field day safety and being kind to others. We go to lunch—ham sandwiches with baby carrots and either a banana or half an apple. Some people are too excited to eat. The teachers save the fruit that people do not eat for others to eat later. Finally, it is time for field day. We gather all of our equipment and line up. My friend and I make sure we are standing close to each other as our whole grade will be outside on the field.

Outside, their are parent volunteers to help with the activities. We decide to skate first. They have cleared the parking lot of cars and marked off a large oval with chalk and small flags. We put on our skates and adjust our knee and elbow pads, tighten our helmet straps and we are ready to go. We do a slower, warm up lap, then go faster. I remember skating at home, my wheels clicking the sidewalk, pulling my brother in his wagon as my father watched from the porch. I hope Momma saved his wagon. We skate until our shins begin to ache and we are hot. We sit down to rest. Just then, a boy from another class comes over and looks at me. Laughing and pointing, he says "You don't have a home. You're homeless!" I don't know what to say. My friend stands up and looks directly at him. "You are so wrong! I went to her house last weekend. You don't know anything! She even has a new puppy." She continues to glare at him and he leaves, mumbling to himself. She looks at me. "Are you OK?" I am numb at first. How can he know? Now he knows and someone else knows and the woman who left Emily knows. If all these people know, someone will find us. My friend reaches out to help me up. "Come on, we can't think about all that. School will be out on Friday. Who is going to listen to him? Tell your Mom. She will take care of it." My friend knows the truth for both of us.

"Come on, let's go."

We run to where the hula hoops are. We laugh as we watch others and then try to do it ourselves, collapsing on the ground in laughter as the hoops first fall to the ground. We try again, determined to do it. We stand too close together and our hoops hit each other. Finally, we get serious and try again. We get them going on the third try, a little bit, then a little bit more. We try to change positions and keep the hoops going. They drop. We try the move again. This is harder than it looks. The volunteer suggests we go get refreshments, and come back if we want to try again.

There are icy, fruity snowcones to turn our lips and tongues blue and orange and red and purple. Soft drinks, we can have one, but we have to get it from our teacher; water and sports drinks and fruit. We get blue snowcones and then a banana to split. We find a shady spot to sit and cool off. I hope Teacup puppy doesn't cry too much or make too much noise or make too much of a mess doing her puppy business in the shed. I wonder what Momma did about Emily. My friend senses my thoughts are far away and says so. I have to come back to now.

We decide to do one race; it is too hot to do more than that. My friend is going to watch me race, then I will watch her jump-rope. Several other kids are already racing. I will be racing a boy who is a little older than me from a different grade. I stand to the side, sizing him up. He doesn't look like he runs or walks on a regular basis. He could just be talented. He turns suddenly and sees me. I turn red and turn away. My friend is giggling. We wait. I retie my shoes to make sure the laces are secure but not too tight. The boy figures out that I am racing him. "You're serious, aren't you," he says. I turn red again. Boys don't usually talk to me except about stupid stuff and I don't encourage them to talk to me. I look straight at him. "Yeah, I'm serious. I like running. I do it for me." Running is one of the few things that I can do, no matter what. I watch the other people race, then it is our turn. I do not look at this boy. I concentrate and focus on my run. I don't have to pace myself for this one, it is just a sprint. Just go. My feet hit the ground and the energy surges through me as though I am flying. I run past the finish line and stop. It felt so good to run. The boy comes up behind me. "Man, you are fast. You blew me away. Good race." He offers to shake hands. I have never shaken hands with a boy like this. I shake hands with him. He grins. "Firm handshake, too. And all this time I've never noticed you. If you want to run and train, I know a team that would love to have you. It's at a church." Then he tells me where they meet and when. I'm sure it's our church - the one where we had the bake sale, where we go. The one whose garden shed we live in. I thank him for the information. "I'll talk to my Mother about it. I think I know where that church is. Thanks for the information." He smiles, says goodbye and leaves. My friend can barely control her giggles until he leaves. Her giggles burst out like the fizz from a shaken can of soda. "Oooo, I think he likes you, he was impressed with how you ran and that you beat him. You were flying." "Being impressed is not the same as liking someone. He doesn't even know my name. I don't know his name and I bet he is two grades ahead of us!"

"Still, he noticed you." I shake my head at her. "Let's go find the jump ropes. I want to watch you jump while I catch my breath." I look at the time. This will probably be the last thing we do before we go home. We turn to go when the parent volunteer stops us, looking at me. My heart begins to race. "Young lady, you had the fastest time I have ever seen and you made it look easy. I clocked you. This medal's for you." I stare at the ribbon and the medal hanging from it. My Dad used to clock me when I ran. I manage to say thank you.

At jump ropes, the parent volunteer is glad to see us. Not too many people have been jumping rope. My friend will need another person to turn the rope, even if I help. The parent volunteer doesn't know how to turn the rope if it is doubled. I look out across the field, searching for people to be rope turners. My friend and I head in opposite directions and will return in 5 minutes.

I have found Yolanda. She and her friends practice all the time.

32

My friend has found, ... has found that boy. That boy?!! The one I raced with. What is she thinking? She is grinning from ear to ear. She knows what she is doing. Man, are we going to talk about this later. The guy looks a little embarrassed. "My little sister does this with her friends. I don't mind helping," he says. He and Yolanda take the ropes, turning slowly at first, then faster. My friend runs in, jumping and turning in a complete circle. A crowd begins to gather, clapping in time and chanting. Rosita asks to run in. My friend moves to let her in, never missing a beat. Rosita runs in and someone starts a song in Spanish that I don't know. The beat picks up. My friend signals she is tired and runs out. All of a sudden, one of the guys runs in. Rosita knows him. The crowd roars. They do a routine, almost like a dance, that my friend and I have never seen. It is beautiful. Everyone claps. They run out and the ropes stop. Everyone claps again. The parent volunteer gives all three of them medals. It is time to collect all of our equipment and go inside. We gather up the ropes and run across the field to get our skates. We will have to walk back. We cannot run with our skates. The air in the building feels good. Our teacher has us to pile all the equipment at the front of the room as she checks it off, after she checks to make sure our class is all there. We sure a sweaty bunch of kids. Some of us definitely need deodorant. I am glad we can at least afford that. Momma always makes sure that I have these kind of things. I sometimes wonder how she does it. She has even let me bring something for my friend before, when her Mother didn't have the money. We can still have something to drink. My friend and I get our soft drinks. The class is allowed to talk softly for the last 10 minutes of class. Our teacher asks for volunteers to put away the equipment. Several of the guys volunteer to help. Tomorrow we will put away our books. Friday is our trip! Then school is over. I cannot wait to get home to see Teacup, even if she has made a mess everywhere. I wish I could go see her instead of going to the cousins' house. I wonder what happened with Emily.

My friend and I walk as far as we can together going home and then we go our separate ways. I so want to go home instead of going to the cousins' house. I am tired and I do want a nap. I can't do that at our garden shed, not during the day. I hope it is quiet at the cousins house. I look forward to our own house, wherever it is and being able to sleep in my own room, with Teacup and my future cat. If I even go by our garden shed, I know I will want to stop, and I can't. I am just too tired.

It is quiet at the cousins' house. I manage to get in and go to the back. I check on my brother, who is sleeping. I flop down on the twin bed and find my comfortable spot, pulling up the sheet around me, getting the pillow just where I want it. Sleep is welcoming. A comfort after a long day. I dream about our new house.

I hear a baby crying, but it is not my brother. It is a baby. Em? I am fully awake. How could I have missed another baby in the room? It is Em. Why is she here? Not that I am sorry to see her, actually. She sees me and holds up her arms, smiling. I smile back and pick her up, she snuggles against me. I still don't see how she is still here. I can't imagine the cousins were too happy to see her. I am sure they will want more money now. She is not wet. I check on my brother and take Em into the kitchen in search of a bottle. She has one mixed up. I heat it in the microwave, test the temperature and talk to her. She smiles and waves her little arms. Her bottle is ready. She reaches out and takes it, sucking vigorously and then stopping. She looks at me and smiles. Em is actually kind of fun. I carry her back to the porch room. I put a blanket down with some toys on it and make sure Em is sitting in a stable position. I set her bottle down beside her and go check on my brother. He is beginning to wake up. I leave him alone for a few more minutes and look over at Em. She is trying to balance and hold her bottle at the same time. She is wobbling. I catch her just in time and hold her while she finishes her bottle. I pat her back and sit her back on the blanket. My brother is awake and starts talking to himself. Em is listening. She answers back. My brother vocalizes louder. It is as though he and Em are having an actual conversation. I get him up and change him, then put him on the blanket with Em.

All is well until he reaches for her toy. She says "No" loudly and snatches the toy back. Em can talk! My brother looks startled and begins to cry. He never expected Em to stand up to him. Now Em starts to cry, too. This can't be good. I sit on the floor with them, one in each arm. I need two more arms. Fortunately, they quiet down. I hope Momma comes home soon.

Being a Mother or a big sister to two babies is hard. I still haven't gotten to eat my snack yet. I have yogurt and a granola bar in my backpack. I put Em and my brother down. They reach for different toys. I am safe. I get up and find my backpack. I am hungry. I open the granola bar first. The crackly paper makes the babies look up. I laugh at them. "You do not have enough teeth for this." I pop the top on the yogurt and the fruit smell tickles my nose. The babies drop their toys and turn to me. "No, now, I need to eat this. Em, Em, you just had a bottle." At the word bottle, my brother looks around. He is getting sippy cups and would rather have a bottle. I dip my granola bar in the yogurt and crunch down, the cold yogurt and the honey nut crunchiness of the granola feel good on my tongue. I close my eyes just for a moment. I hear little bodies crawling towards me. I quickly open my eyes. I am under attack. I hold up my snack and start trying to get up. I manage to set it on the dresser behind me, before they get to me. Thankfully, I hear the door. "Mom, help! They're ganging up on me. How did you manage to keep Em?" My Mother laughs at the situation, as my brother abruptly turns and begins crawling toward Momma. That's fine with me. I do not want to be Momma.

Momma bends down and picks up my brother. Em watches and crawls to me. "All right, little girl. I'll hold you but I still get to eat." She crawls into my lap and leans against me. Momma settles onto the floor across from me with my brother. She asks how my day was and I tell her everything, even about the boy saying I was homeless and beating the other boy in the race. She listens. Momma is always good about listening. She asks if I'm OK and is there anything else that she can do. I'd like to tell her I really want a house, our own place, but I can't say that. Momma is just looking at me. She knows that I want to say more. "Sweetheart, we will have our own place. I want it, too. I want it, too."

35

It was like Momma can read my mind or I guess my heart. I can read other people, too, sometimes. Momma says its a gift, that you have to use it wisely and for good. Then she says, "Well, was the boy in the race cute?" "Mom!" I say, turning red. "Dear daughter, it is normal to notice boys and what they look like. I noticed your Father was cute. Actually, your Father is downright handsome, wherever he is right now." I do not want to think about my Father right now and Momma can't think about him either, not really. We have too much to do. But I want to know about Emily. "Momma, what about Emily? How does she still get to be here?" Momma takes a deep breath and kisses the top of my brother's head. "When I get to work, the papers were there in an envelope for me. I called the HOW. She came on my break. We talked. Because the Mother gave us Emily, it is different than she just abandoned her. The only problem is where we live. We are going to have to find another place to live. But for now, she will stay with us. Our worker will get her added to our food stamps and get her added to the child care. The cousins are happy about the extra money. The only thing is—are you OK with it? It's also going to be extra work and responsibility for you." Momma looks at me for an answer. "And, yes, we are keeping the puppy. I have food for her." I had almost forgotten about her. I have a puppy, my puppy. Not Momma's or Daddy's or my little brother's or Em's. Mine! Mine! Mine! Mine! Momma is still waiting for an answer. She knows I have been thinking of something else. Do I want a baby sister? Em snuggles closer and looks up at me. I stroke her springy curls. Can I deal with a baby sister, a baby brother and my puppy? School is about over. That part is good. I won't have to deal with the boy who said I was homeless. I'll be going to summer camp. I'll only have to be a big sister to them in the afternoons and on the weekends. Momma will be there, too, and eventually Daddy. It's not like Momma is going to dump them on me and be gone forever like happens to my friends sometimes. One girl at school has to watch her brothers and sisters all the time, even on weekends. School is her only break. Momma wouldn't do that to me. OK, I've kept Momma waiting long enough. "I can do it, Momma. I can handle a baby sister and a baby brother." Em looks at me as if she knows. Now she has a family, too.

The cousins interrupt by banging on the door. "Are we going to eat or not?" Momma laughs and rolls her eyes. I giggle and the babies laugh, too.

We each pick up a baby and head to the kitchen. Momma brings out a second baby backpack. She puts my brother in his and shows me how to put Em in hers. We put Em in and Momma helps me to tighten the straps. I can't see Em but Momma says she is smiling. "The only thing you have to be careful about is bending over and the baby grabbing things. When you bend over, Em can slide forward and bump her head. Be careful about what she grabs. Now we're having spaghetti. Do you want to do salads or meat, sauce, noodles?"

"Em and I will do salads." I open the refrigerator and Em giggles. She likes riding on my back. She immediately reaches for the butter and the eggs. "No, Em." She takes her little hands back. Em is such a sweet, loving child. How could her Mother ever give her up?

I take out celery, tomatoes, carrots, romaine lettuce and iceberg lettuce. Mom hands me a small box of spinach leaves and a boiled egg for each salad. I set all the bowls out and begin chopping carrots and celery. I tear the lettuce and put both kinds in each bowl, topping it with spinach leaves. Then I add the other vegetables, arranging the tomatoes and sliced eggs in a pattern on the top. Finally, I sprinkle cheese over everything. I move to tend the noodles. I can do this part, too, while Momma makes the meat sauce. Em is moving around to get a better look at the steam. "It is hot, Em, don't touch it." She moves her little hands back and just watches. The smell of the meat cooking with the onions and green peppers fills the air. We will have a kitchen, our own kitchen, with Momma's cast iron pans. A refrigerator with food in it that is ours and a special place for my chocolate drinks. I won't have to hide my snacks for after school. Momma interrupts my thoughts. "Precious One, I think the noodles have cooked enough. Drain them, please." I can easily imagine Momma at the restaurant. I know she's not calling them Precious One, but I'm

37

sure she gets things done). I sure could use a piece of peanut butter cake or some peach cobbler, even before dinner. I bet Em would like it, too. She and my brother are going to be messy spaghetti eaters. Momma puts her fingers to her lips and motions me to the side, pointing to a sack. I peek inside. The rich chocolate aroma greets me. Chocolate fudge cake. Ohhh! Wonderful! But we will have to share it. I could eat mine now. Momma made it just for us, not the restaurant. When Momma makes it just for us, it is like having a kitchen.

I set the table and let the cousins know that dinner is ready. Em claps her hands as though she understands. I take Em out of her backpack. We all sit down. Em has a little plate next to mine. We have the blessing. I cut her spaghetti into little bites. She wants the spoon. I give her a piece of garlic bread. She sniffs it and touches the buttery part with her fingers and then puts her fingers in her mouth. Finally, she takes a bite of it. She chews it. She likes it. She swallows it and reaches for her bottle. I offer her a bite of spaghetti. She takes it. Then I get another bite and give her the spoon. She gives it back. That will work. It will save my school uniform. I feed Em all of her spaghetti and she finishes off the bread; I help her hold her bottle while I pour dressing on my salad. Momma has let my brother feed himself while he sits in his highchair. He even got to have some thin, raw carrot slices. He is eyeing Em's bottle. Momma hands him his cup. Em watches me eat salad. She laughs when I crunch carrots and celery. The spaghetti is so good, I understand why she liked the bread. I sit back against the chair. Em is getting sleepy. I help Momma clear the table by stacking plates while I'm still sitting and holding Em. And we still have that wonderful, delicious chocolate cake. Momma gets her coffee and sets it down beside me with the dessert plates and a knife, out of Em's reach. Then she brings out the cake. She cuts a piece for everyone, even my brother. She lets me cut my own. Even the cousins are complimentary. "Max, you really outdid yourself tonight. I see why people pay for that chocolate cake." That is probably the nicest thing they have ever said to Momma. She smiles back. "I'm really glad you liked it."

Em is asleep. Momma takes her from my arms and puts her in the back room. She finishes her coffee and refills her cup. Now it is time to clean the kitchen. There is no spaghetti or salad left. She cuts the cake in half and wraps it in foil, then hands it to me. I go back to get our things together and get the babies.

I am tired and we still have to walk home. Momma comes back to help me. We double check to make sure we have everything. We pack the strollers and load the babies. Em is sound asleep. My brother watches her sleep. He always likes the walk home. The cousins actually say goodnight. Usually they just ignore us as we leave. One of them holds the door and helps me get Em and stroller out. I tell him thank you. What did Momma put in that cake and the spaghetti?

The night is warm, but not hot. The stars are out. The fan will feel good. Teacup. I still have to clean up puppy poop. Momma look at me and smiles, reading my mind. "I'll help. Let's just get the babies settled first. I'll put them to bed while you take Teacup outside. Don't walk very far into that field. I'll give you a flashlight."

We stop at the gas station. Momma has brought the guy at the station a piece of cake. Momma said he works at night to help pay for going to college. Momma said it's also good advertising for the restaurant. She gives him one of the restaurant's cards. I am full from dinner. I do not want anything. I do use the restroom again while Momma waits with the babies. The guy gave Momma all of the old newspapers. We will use them for Teacup and the babies. Great! Puppy potty papers and leaky diapers. We are almost to our street. We check to make sure that no one is following us. We walk down the street in the quiet of the night. Suddenly, the silence is broken by the noise of joyful puppy barks as we approach the shed. Teacup is throwing herself against the door. She comes bounding out into my arms. She runs in circles, stopping to do her business in the grass. Momma checks the shed. Teacup has messed only once in the corner. Momma gives me the other flashlight to track Teacup as she runs around. Momma cleans up the one mess in the corner, while I feed Teacup and give her water. Momma and I check for stray bugs and spiders, then put my brother and Em to bed. Now we can go to bed.

Teacup is crying and scratching the door; she wants to get out. It is early, not quite time to get up. I disentangle myself from Em, making sure not to wake her up. I open the door to look out but Teacup scampers out and down the steps. I sit on the top step and watch her run through the grass. I think about how it will be when we have a backyard. Teacup comes up and sits on my feet. I cuddle her in my lap and rub my face against her soft curly fur. Then we go back in. We have almost an hour left to sleep.

The alarm goes off. Teacup barks sleepy little puppy barks. I gather her up, stepping carefully. We are going back outside. I walk down the steps and deposit her wiggly, curly self in the grass. She runs off a ways and turns to look at me. I look the other way as she does her business, then I clean it up for the trash. She follows close at my heels. Today should be an easy day at school. We are packing up our books. We will only have worksheets and our final test in reading/English and math. I pick up Teacup and rub her gently. She grunts and tries to lick my face. I take her back in and show her the corner with the puppy papers. Further over are her food and water dishes. She sticks her front paws in the water dish and gets a drink. Her ears get wet. She wags her tail about the food. I have to hurry and get dressed because I have to get Em ready. While Teacup happily crunches her breakfast, I choose an outfit for Emily - pale yellow, lightweight cotton pants and a short sleeved yellow flowered shirt. Em still wants to sleep. She doesn't care if I change her clothes but she is not happy about getting her face washed and her hands cleaned. She also gets a clean diaper. I put a jacket on her and lay her in the stroller. She goes back to sleep. I wish I could sleep longer, too. Momma has my brother ready and we have to start moving out. I gather my backpack and Em's bag. Momma helps me get the stroller down the steps. I help her get my brother down the steps. Teacup waits in the doorway. I give her one last pat on the head, then down her back. She moves out of the way as I shut the door and lock it, handing the keys over to Momma. We are ready.

As we get close to the school, Momma puts Em and my brother in the same stroller. Em doesn't care. Momma folds up Em's stroller. I kiss everyone goodbye. Em is still sleeping. Momma gives me a hug and lets me go. I only have one more day after this one. I turn and walk towards the school. My friend is waiting.

My friend gave her Mother the information about the job and her Mother applied already. She will start work on Friday. They are moving to their new apartment this weekend. My friend will have her own room. Then I can come visit her this summer. We should be getting a place, too.

For breakfast, there is blueberry muffins and sausage. I get chocolate milk even though it doesn't really go well with blueberry muffins. I just really like chocolate milk. The milk is cold and the muffins are hot. The whole cafeteria has a blueberry smell, so much better than how it smells sometimes. My friend is so excited about having a real home again. Now she will be able to enjoy the rain. We will have to have a place that lets you have dogs.

It is hard to wait and be quiet while everyone turns in their books. Some students don't have all of their books. If you don't turn in all of your books, you have to pay for them before you can get your report card. I worked hard to keep my books in good condition and not have them get wet when it rained. I read my library book (from the church library) while we wait. My friend is drawing. She has all of her books, too. One boy is starting to cry. The other boys are making fun of him. He doesn't have all of his books. He says they went to a restaurant where they all had dinner with his grandfather, to celebrate his Grandfather's birthday and there was this really wonderful chocolate cake. At the mention of chocolate cake, I know what restaurant he went to. I raise my hand and ask to speak to him. I tell him that I know where his books are if he left them at the restaurant where they have "really wonderful chocolate cake." He stops crying. "How do you know?" he asks. "Because my Mother is the one who makes the chocolate cake. I had some last night after dinner. I'll ask her about your books tonight. She will know where they are." The boy is relieved. My teacher does

41

not want to wait until tomorrow to find the books. She calls the restaurant and makes the boy ask about his books. They do have them. The restaurant will hold them so that his Mother can pick them up. Then my teacher asks about buying a chocolate cake. A whole cake, not just several pieces. The restaurant is happy to sell her a cake. She will pick it up tomorrow after school.

It is my turn to check in my books. My teacher compliments me on the good condition of my books. She says she will be looking forward to getting her chocolate cake. I wonder who will be helping her to eat it. My friend turns in her books. She kept hers in plastic, too. The teacher compliments her, also. We are homeless and we managed to take care of our books better than anyone else. What the world doesn't know, so much, so much.

We get our workbooks for math and reading. We will take them home with us but tear out today's pages. These will be our last grades. My grades have been good, some have been excellent. Those afternoons in the library before I went to the cousins' house have paid off. Momma had gotten me some old business cards that were blank on the back. They made great cards for vocabulary/spelling and math formulas. I even used them for Spanish class. I also had enough to share with my friend. It helped her with her grades, too. Business cards are a great size because they fit so easy in your pocket. You can pull them out and study anywhere, except if you're in the dark. Then you can just think until you have too many thoughts and you have to go to sleep to escape. Sometimes sleep is the only escape.

Now we are supposed to read, then do the vocabulary and answer the questions. The selection is from a book I have already read but that is OK. It is not hard to match up the vocabulary words and the definitions. The questions take longer but I get them done and tear them out of my book. Now I can read my library book until lunch time. We are going to eat our lunch outside under the trees. Oh, wait, my teacher wants me. She wants me to help people who aren't finished with their work. Well, I guess I can. I would rather read my library book. That may be selfish of me but that is what I'd rather do. I am helping someone in our class that I do not know really well. She is small and quiet and Hispanic. I feel really tall around her. She is having trouble with reading English. She can read a little bit, but not much. She understands much more than she can read. She says she reads Spanish really well. Some of the students do not read Spanish or English. Some of them have to be the family translator. My Momma and I are learning Spanish. I help my classmate to read the pages. She knows the answers if I read the words and the questions. Some of her answers to the questions are better answers than mine. I really like her. Somehow, I sense she would be easy to talk to and that she would understand. Maybe she has been through some of the same things my friend and I have been through. We finish the assignment. I am hungry. As we get our things together, I quickly ask my friend if the Hispanic girl can join us. I know we will be safe. She agrees. We get our lunches and ask her if she would like to join us. She hesitates at first, then says yes. We find a spot in the shade away from the boys. It is not yet the really hot part of the day. Some of the lunches have ham sandwiches, some of them have chicken. We all have chicken, chips, an apple, cheese and crackers, a cookie and milk. We try to speak Spanish, our new friend is laughing. We are saying different different words than we think we are saying. We decide we will all speak English. I tell her about my new puppy and about Em. She, too, is surprised that we get to keep Em. She says her family had to live with relatives before, too, and it was really crowded. It was easier for her to find a place to sleep because she is small but sometimes she did not always get enough to eat. If the meat ran out, her Mother would share hers or just give it to her. My Mother has done that, too. We talk about tomorrow and what we are going to ride. I am glad that there are three of us, it will be safe.

As we get ready to go back to class, some other girls come up to us. They are talking to our new friend in rapid fire Spanish. I understand very little of what they are saying, only that our friend looks ready to cry. Something is wrong. I need to do something, to stand up for her. "Please, I do not know what is wrong, only that you are upset.

We want to be friends. Amigas. We can be friends even if our language is not the same." I look at them and put my arms around my friends' shoulders. I am the tallest. The other girls look at us and at each other. They join arms with us and we stand together. "Friends, Amigas. Juntos. Together." The bell rings; laughing, we join hands and run for the door.

Math is next. The teacher says this assignment will add extra points to our grade if we need them and just improve our grade otherwise. My grades are good, we've had lunch, maybe my stomach can withhot now. This is all stuff that we have had; I can do some of the calculation in my head. I make a game of calculating it in my head before I work the answers and show my work. I check my answers with the calculator and turn in my papers. I will have to do math this summer so I don't forget anything. Reading is the easy part. Now I get to read my library book. Finally, everyone is finished. Math is done for the year! At school anyway. I am going to find some fun ways to use math this summer.

I am hoping we get to do another art project. Yay, we do! The teacher has chenille sticks. She says that years ago, they only came in white and were called pipe cleaners. They were used to clean pipes that people smoked. Yuck! She shows us a name written in cursive. Then she shows us the name made from chenille stems in cursive. First, we write our names or the word we have chosen to do, in cursive. Our teacher checks them and makes suggestions for how to do the letters and how to connect them. We choose our colors and begin forming our letters, cutting the chenille pieces with scissors as we need to. Writing in cursive is much easier than forming the letters. We get to talk quietly while we work. Some of the people are getting frustrated. Someone balls up their chenille stems and throws them on the floor. They land in a mangled wad of color beside my desk. I pick them up and set them at the corner of my desk. Maybe I can help them later. They did pick good colors that go well together.

My friend, Katherine, and I finish our names, then we get extra stems to decorate with. The balled up stems are still on my desk; I look around to see who they belong to. I cannot tell. Katherine and I began to untangle them. The letters look like they should spell Mother. She takes part of them and I take part of them. We make the letters, we join them together and add flowers and leaves. It is beautiful. I lay it flat on my desk. We get a break and go to the restroom. When we get back, the name is gone. I hope that the right person took it. In some ways, I wish that I had done my Mother's name also. The teacher calls us up to her desk and tells us thank you. She says the right person got the name. We tell her that she is welcome. I would like to have art every day, but I will have to wait until I go to high school. I do it every day on my own in some way. Tomorrow, tomorrow, we'll play all day tomorrow— to borrow from the Annie song. My teacher thanks us again and we sit down. It is almost time to go home. We gather up our papers and workbooks to take home. I put mine in my book bag. The bell rings. We can go. I have made it through the school year. My secret is still safe. To the cousins' house and Em and my baby brother and then home to Teacup. Katherine and I get ready to walk home. As we go out, all of the Hispanic girls are waiting. They smile shyly and come toward us. One of the girls speaks to us in Spanish. The girl I helped, Lourdes, translates. "We are all friends, we are all sisters." Smiles need no translation. We are all talking, Spanish, English bits and parts of both. No one else walks the way we do, so we will still be walking by ourselves. But we will see them tomorrow. We exchange hugs and say goodbye. I wish that we had become friends earlier in the year.

Katherine and I begin our walk home. Her new home apartment will still be this way. She shows me the apartment building and gives me her new address. Her aunt is already there, getting things ready. She is going home. She gives me a hug and we head our separate ways. My snacks are in my backpack.

I am almost to the cousins' house when I see them. From down the street I see. Police cars, three of them! What is wrong? I want to run to the house, I want to check on Em and my brother. I want to run away. Momma needs to be here. I need Momma. I call Momma at work. She answers right away; she knows it is me. I tell her what I see. She will call the cousins and call me back. I wait.

Forever. It is not about us, she says, it is about them. One of them is being arrested for back child support and questioning about a gun. I feel sorry for the child for them having a parent like that and no, they get too angry to have a gun. Still, I will wait until the police are gone. I am a little early yet to be here. Where will I go? I turn to go when I hear a car and a familiar voice. A woman gets out and calls my name. It is our HOW. I walk over to her car. "It is alright. Your Mother called me. I will wait with you. I want to tell you about the camp I found. I know you are scared. Do you want a hug?"

All of a sudden I am crying and I cannot hold all of it in. Ms. Jackson gives me lots of soft tissues. She lets me cry and talk. We go to the store and she buys me a soft drink. I feel better. She says she understands about holding things in and then letting go. We talk about camps and Em and my baby brother. She asks me about what kind of place I want to live in. I tell her and I also tell her about Teacup. She says she will find us a place that will take Teacup. I am tired and yawning. We drive back to the cousins' house. The police are gone. She walks me to the door and makes sure I get in. I tell her thank you. She gives me a business card with all of her phone numbers. I put it with Momma's card. She leaves and I lock the door. The house is quiet. I walk to the back. Blessing, blessing. The babies are still sleeping. I curl into my bed and relish this time.

I awaken to ... my Momma's voice. "Hello, Precious One. I'm sorry you had such a rough beginning to your afternoon. I was scared, too. I love you." She gathers me into her arms for a hug. It feels safe to be in my Momma's arms. "I love you, too, Momma." The babies are waking up. I stretch and relax. Time to get up. I put on my shoes and amble over to Em's crib. She opens her eyes, smiles at me and squeals. "Em, Em you are stinky. We will have to make you more socially acceptable." How can babies do this gross stuff? She laughs. Momma offers to change her since it is stinky. But I will be brave. I will do it. At least she will not spray like my brother does sometimes. Yuck, yuck, yuck. Several wipes later, we have a clean baby. Now I can pick her up. Momma has my brother and the baby snacks. I have Em and my snacks. We sit on the floor. Momma sits across from me. I tell her about my ~~date~~ visit with Ms. Jackson, our HOW and that she is looking at houses for us. Momma says we may take the babies on Saturday and walk around the neighborhood to look for houses. We could have a picnic lunch before she has to go to the restaurant for a few hours. I tell her about my day at school and making friends with the Hispanic girls. Momma says we did the right thing. That sometimes when ~~people are ostraci~~ people are ostracized, left out, and someone tries to befriend someone in that group, their own group may turn against ~~them~~ for offering or accepting friendship. She is glad it turned out OK. When we get a house, I can have friends over to visit and then to spend the night.

It is time to start dinner. We are having baked chicken, baked apples, baked potatoes and green beans. The chicken is ready to start I am going to watch the beans and the apples. Momma has already cut the beans and the apples. We will put the potatoes in with the chicken. I wrap the potatoes in foil and place them in ~~the~~ the oven beside the chicken. Em and my brother are in their highchairs away from the oven. I think they like their backpacks better but the oven is too hot for them to be near it. I could not bend over with Em in the backpack, check the oven and keep her safe. The kitchen gets hot and Momma turns on the fan. The babies notice and clap their hands, briefly watching the fan. Em is out of cereal bits and reaches over for some of my brother's. He looks at her, looks at me and decides his strategy. He moves some to the side out of her reach and some closer to her. Then he grins. Em is happy and smiles back. Momma takes out some green beans to cool. They can eat those by themselves. My brother eagerly eats his. Em pokes them and slides them around the tray like cars or boats. Finally, she eats one. She likes it. She begins making all kinds of sounds. My brother begins answering and waiting for her reply. I love to hear them do this. All of sudden, Em looks at me and at Momma. She is making m and ma sounds. "Mmmm, maaa- Mama!" Em is delighted with

herself. "Oh, wonderful, Little One, yes, we will be Momma to you."
I do not mind sharing my Momma with Em. I still cannot get
over how she came to be with us. Now my brother and Em are banging
their trays, chanting "Mama" in rhythm. Who knew babies could
do rhythm like that! Dinner is about done. I quickly set the table
and fix up little plates for Em and my brother. I move the highchairs
out of the kitchen and to the table. I make sure Em's food is close
to mush. My brother can chew, he's got teeth. As usual, dinner is
quickly gone. The apples are still hot and melt in my mouth. I blow
on Em's to cool them off. She is definitely interested. She lets me
feed her apples and mushy potatoes with chicken. My brother makes
a mess but eats all of his dinner and part of Momma's. She doesn't
mind. There are a lot of dishes to wash and clean up. Now we can
backpack babies. They enjoy clean up time. And tomorrow is my
play day. In a short time, Momma and I have everything done.
We head to the backroom to pack. I can tell that Em is already
asleep. I am going to leave her in her backpack. I get my clothes
for tomorrow and make sure I have my lunch money, my sunblocker.
I get all of Em's things. How can babies be so little and need so
much stuff? I get her favorite toy from under the chair and we are
ready to go. I am so tired. Em feels heavy tonight. Momma and I
head out the door. We are not to far down the street when I hear
someone call my name. They are walking towards us. It is my new
friend from school, Lourdes, and her Mother. She speaks to us in English
and then translates for her Mother. Her Mother says the babies are
beautiful. She offers us a ride home. Lourdes sees the look on my
face and quickly explains that we want to walk. I tell her I am
looking forward to tomorrow and that we have to go. She says yes,
it is getting late. We say goodbye. Then Lourdes turns back and
runs after us, excited. "There is a house near here. It is small, 3
bedrooms and only one bathroom. But it is clean. It has a yard with a
fence and grass. The kitchen is good. My uncle owns it. He had to
take a job in another city, away from us. You will look at it?"
My heart jumps. This more than I can hope for. I can tell Momma
feels the same way, she finds words to speak as I am still trying to

process the information. "We will look at it. We would be pleased to see it. Thank you for your kindness." Lourdes beams a sunlight smile in the darkness. She understands. We hug each other good bye. The journey home is shorter. We stop at the gas station and I do not even unload Em. Teacup and bedtime, bedtime. Momma asks "Precious, I will have some money tomorrow. Will it bother you if I go look at the house before I see you and if it is good, I will put money down on it to hold it for us?" "Well, I guess not, Momma, but I really want to see it with you. What if I meet you at the restaurant right after school? Lourdes and her Mother can drop me off."
"OK, sweetie, I know this is important to you. Let's meet right after school. I can't believe we may have a house."

We are up to our little house and Teacup is whimpering happy puppy noises. Momma lets me unlock the door. Teacup rushes out into my arms, then running in circles around us. She darts for the bushes. Teacup likes her privacy. Momma takes my brother in. I sit on the steps in the open doorway and wait. Teacup bounds up the steps, a letter in her mouth. It is from the church. I gather up TCee and give the letter to Momma. "Momma, TCee found this letter!"
Momma takes the letter, studies it and opens it. She reads it. She is laughing and crying as she hands me the letter and the flashlight. I quickly scan the letter. I am laughing, too. They are inviting us to church. We already go to church with them, they just don't know it. Well, maybe they do know we are here. But we haven't damaged the shed. In fact, we improved it. We've cleaned it on a regular basis, the door has a good lock now. We added pretty curtains and all the windows work. They have screens and wrought iron burglar bars. Teacup is barking! I manage to grab her as Momma slams the door shut and locks it. Double dead bolt. Voices! Someone is coming. Men! I have heard these voices before at the cousins' house. I do not like them. As Momma locks the door, I see the glint of a metal door, mounted behind our wooden door. It has a red ribbon on it. Our worker put us up a security door, just where we need it, on the inside. Using the flashlight, I threw the latches and lock the door. Even if the wooden door breaks, the steel door will hold.

I turn on my tape recorder and place it behind the door in the corner. The men are laughing outside the door. "That little old wooden door won't keep us out. We came to get some of that new check your husband's been sending and get some dessert. Maybe some you made, maybe some you get. I been wanting to sample that little tall girl, too."

I am terrified. Momma motions for me to move the babies to one side with Teacup. I place them away from the windows. Momma is angry, but deadly calm. There is something different about her. She moves to a space between the windows and opens a small door that I have never seen before, taking out something. Does Momma have a gun? I find my cell phone to call the police. At least now I know the address. The men are kicking the door, harder and harder. They sound drunk. The door is holding. I call 911. I try not to scream and to talk slow enough for them to understand. "Please help us, send the police now! Men are trying to break into our house. They are drunk. They say they have a gun. The address is No, it is not a house. Yes we live here. It's the garden shed behind the gray stone First Cumberland Presbyterian Church. Linden, the street behind the church. Yes, I'm sure. Just come. They are breaking the windows!" The woman wants me to stay on the line. I'm crying. All of a sudden, I remember Betsy's rocks. I don't know who Betsy is or was, but I have her rocks. I pick up one as a hand comes through the glass. I smash the rock against the hand as hard as I can. A man howls and curses. I fumble in the box in the corner. Rat trap. Carefully I set the trap. A hand comes through the window. The trap snaps shut. Two damaged hands, lots of cursing. The trap bangs against the window as he writhes in pain. The wrist looks broken, swelling. The babies are crying, Teacup is barking, glass is breaking, glass is breaking. They stop for a minute. "B——, you better open the door before we break it." More cursing. A hand comes through the door again. I miss. I set the bigger trap. The hand comes through and into the trap. The trap catches but does not clamp shut. He tries to withdraw his hand. The trap clamps down hard. He cannot withdraw his hand. He kicks the door. He bangs his captured hand against the door and drops to the steps in agony. Suddenly, I see a blur of white. ~~Two of~~ Two of the biggest dogs that I've ever seen. Two large white dogs come bounding up, one is limping, bleeding. God has sent us angel dogs. They attack the men, pouncing on them. The one at the door is captive, he cannot get away and the dog is biting him hard. This man has done something to this dog. The other man is not doing any better. "I thought you shot the dog. There was only one. When we whacked old Ms. Bessie." I know that name. Ms. Bessie. Old Ms. Bessie, gentle sweet Ms. Bessie at church. I'm talking to the 911 operator again. She asks, "What are you doing, what is going on?" "Not now," I say. "These men have hurt someone else." I scramble in the darkness and find the old, old church directory. Ms. Bessie probably still lives in the old family home. I flip through the brittle yellow pages, cannot worry about tears in pages. The end, the W's. I give them her address and tell them to hurry. Now there is only the sounds of the dogs snapping and snarling, and the men yelling and crying out. If they would be still, the dogs might stop biting them. Suddenly, it is quiet. Only the babies crying and Teacup barking. The police are here. I hear an officer and see a bright light. The man at the door is yelling. "Officer, help us. This woman and her b____ kid tried to kill us. We came to visit. They sicced ~~thier~~ their dogs on us..." The officer is laughing. I look out the door. The dog is laying square on the man's back, he is spreadeagled on the ground, one hand in a trap. The dog wags his tail at the officer. The man tries to move, the dog growls. The officer takes a photo with his phone. "Evidence." The officer tells the dog. "Good job, Old Jasper." Miss Bessie will be proud of you. You're a hero. We'll take it from here." Old Jasper moves while the officer cuffs the man. The other dog is no where to be seen. The operator is talking to me again. "Honey, are you OK? Are the police there?" I had forgotten about her. "Yes, ma'am. They're here. We're fine. Momma's going to open the door. Bye." Momma holds me in her arms. The officer is talking. "Ma'am, are you all right? Do you need an ambulance? Can you open the door, what's left of it?" Momma answers. "We're fine. I'm going to try to open the door." We undo the latches on the steel door. Momma unlocks the wooden door. The man screams in pain and finally pulls his hand, trap and all from the

51

broken window. He falls in a heap at the bottom of the steps. Teacup stands on the threshold and barks at him. I snatch her up and let the tears flow for a minute into her silky, curly hair. She snuggles against me. The man still says they weren't planning to do anything. I tell the officer about Ms. Bessie. The man says they didn't say it. I know they did. In all the noise, I forgot about the tape. It is still behind the door. Keeping a firm grip on Teacup, I retrieve my little tape recorder. The officer looks at me, curious. My hand shakes a little as I push the play button. The chaos begins again on the tape. I fast forward and there it is. His chilling remark. I stop the tape, remove it and hand it to the officer. "Did they send an officer to go check on Miss Bessie? I gave them her address." Before he can answer, other cars and officers arrive. I recognize one of them from church. "Hon, you saved Miss Bessie. Looks like old Jasper helped you out over here, let me see about him." Jasper is bleeding, he's tired. They put him in the patrol car to take him to the vet. The officer comes back. "Where are you folks staying tonight? Miss Bessie and her housekeeper, Ms. Sanders, want you to come stay at Miss Bessie's. She'll be fine with your little dog. How many babies are we talking about?" I hold up 2 fingers. Momma and I each run grab a baby. Both of them have wet, red faces from crying. They are exhausted. We are exhausted. We don't know Miss Bessie well but we will be safe there. We can bring Teacup. We can't go to the cousins. The police are going there to talk to them, too, and see what they knew. Momma says yes. We can't leave yet. We still have to talk to the officers. I want to say goodbye to Jasper before he goes.

Jasper wags his tail. I pet him and hug him, I scratch his head. He licks Teacup. Em makes noises to him. Then we get out of the car so that he can go to the vet. We are going to sit in another car. I tell the officers everything I know about the men and answer all of their questions as best I can. Em goes to sleep. Teacup goes to sleep. I give them Ms. Jackson's phone number. I tell them about the program and what she does. They ask about school. I give them all of that information. They cannot put us in foster care because we have a HOW and Miss Bessie has offered us housing for the night. We are all well fed and clean. I have good grades and good school attendance. I explain where my Daddy is. I let them know the address of the house we are looking at tomorrow. They ask about the traps. I feel bad about really hurting the men but I had no choice. Each of them has a broken hand/wrist. Actually, the police are pleased, even impressed. The traps were rusty, but solid, like the door, they held. I am almost falling asleep. Finally, we can go. We gather our things and pile into the patrol car to go to Miss Bessie's. One final question - Momma and I, as well as the men, saw two dogs. Miss Bessie now has one dog, Jasper. She used to have two. The other dog's name was Juno. Juno died last year. But there, in the officer's hand, is a dog tag. It says "Juno" and has Miss Bessie's address and phone number on it. He found it on the steps. The man's gun was under the steps. The other dog was truly an angel dog. I am going to look for white feathers when we come back in the daylight. Momma makes sure the door is locked.

Miss Bessie's house is just as I imagined it. Victorian, gingerbread trim, wraparound porch, big yard, old oak trees, wrought iron fence. Miss Bessie had to spend the night at the hospital. Ms. Sanders is waiting. She thanks me for calling the police for Miss Bessie. She shows us where the bathroom is and the kitchen. She offers to fix us a snack. Cold water would be good. She gets me a glass and I sit at the kitchen table with Em still on my back and drink my water. Now I can sleep. Ms. Sanders offers to take Em. I guess I look pretty worn out. I let her take Em. She shows us the bedroom. It is a large room with a double bed and a smaller bed. Not quite a twin, bigger than crib size. Ms. Sanders says it is a special children's bed called a youth bed; it is for Em and my brother. Air conditioning and a ceiling fan, a comfy mattress and clean covers with no danger of bugs, earthly heaven. We bed down the babies. They look happy and ~~fear~~ peaceful together in the youth bed. Teacup is crying softly in her carrier. It has been rough for her, too. I take her out of the carrier and out the front door. Ms. Sanders goes with me, she likes Teacup. We sit on the steps and wait. Teacup does not take long to finish her business and come running back. Briefly, I flash back to earlier in the night when I took her out and I shudder. In the moonlight, Teacup gives a big puppy yawn. Ms. Sanders and I both laugh. It feels good to laugh, after the night that we have had. We are safe. Ms. Sanders asks if she can carry Teacup in; I do not think Teacup will mind, she is very loving. Miss Bessie has not had a little dog in a long time, just Jasper and Juno. Ms. Sanders makes sure we know where everything is before we say goodnight. I thank her for everything and take Teacup into the bedroom. Momma has left a lamp on for me and I get undressed. Teacup always sleeps next to me. I pick her up and plop her onto the bed. She rubs against Momma's back before nuzzling her ear. Momma reaches over and pets her. T wags her tail and kisses my face as I lay down. I could sleep in this bed forever. Momma turns over and kisses me goodnight. "I love you, Precious One. Lots and lots, forever and ever." "I love you, too, Momma. I love you, too."

The next morning, I have slept too late! The sun is up and out and I am not! Momma is up, the babies are up. Teacup and I are late. How could they let me sleep? I throw on my clothes, gather up sleepy Teacup and rush out of the bedroom. "Momma, I'm late." She and Ms. Sanders and the babies are in the kitchen. "Precious, it is all right. Ms. Sanders will take you to school. I have already called them. It is OK. Now, eat some breakfast."

"Let me take T out. I still need to do my hair. Last night seems so far away. But I know it happened. Awful as it was, terrifying as it was, I know it happened. Teacup and I head out the front door. This is such a beautiful house, I cannot take it all in. Even the sunlight streaming in the windows fills me with hope and wonder. Teacup stops to sniff something on the floor in the pool of sunlight, something white. It is a beautiful, soft, silky feather. I smile and pick it up. We go out to the porch. Teacup runs down the steps and the walkway, exploring the yard, before finding the right spot behind a bush. Using the plastic sack, I bag her business. The trash cart is on the side of the house. Teacup likes running around this big yard. Today will be a great day at the park. The park.

"Teacup, you can't dawdle. I have fun waiting for today. People playtime." Who is keeping her today? I eat breakfast in a hurry. I let Momma brush my hair while I eat and put it up so that I won't be hot. Yes, I have the sunblocker. I have done my own hair for a long time; I can tell that Momma really wants to do my hair today, so I let her. Ms. Sanders has packed me some extra snacks. I put them in my backpack with my favorite hat. I go brush my teeth. I am totally ready. I kiss the babies goodbye. Kiss and hug Momma. Pick up Teacup one more time. Ms. Sanders gets her keys and we are out the door. I tell Ms. Sanders thank you for breakfast and making sure that I get to school. I am not quite sure how to get there from here, since we came in the dark. I try to remember the route. Ms. Sanders says that she will pick me up this afternoon. I thank her again; my friends should be waiting.

I run to the door and walk to the office. They give me an admit to class, everyone is waiting, patiently. Some people are reading, some are drawing. Some are driving everyone else nuts by tapping and fidgeting. My teacher is glad to see me. She smiles and shakes her head. I cannot believe everything that has happened since yesterday. I can hardly wait until we can go. Some students still have to turn in books from yesterday. I get out my sketch book and work on drawings of Teacup.

I hope Jasper comes back today and Miss Bessie. Soon it is time to go. The bus is here. The teacher fastens wrist bands on us; she to ride the rides and the other to identify what school we are from. There will be other schools there, too. Lourdes and Katherine and I grab a seat together, we are surrounded by the other Hispanic girls. It feels safe. The teacher counts everyone, makes sure we all have our money. The bus starts up, finally we are going. Some of the students are singing, everyone else seems to be talking at once. It does not take more than 20 minutes to get to the park. The bus drives between the two concrete columns and pulls up to the entrance. The teacher makes us wait while she reviews our instructions. We each have to have a partner or two, no one can be by themselves. One of the partners has to have a watch to keep up with time and get everyone back to the bus on time.

I am the timekeeper for us. The teacher stops talking. No one has questions. She moves down the aisle and out the door. Without running, we move as quickly as we can off the bus. Now we can run.

We grab a map; what should we ride first? Lourdes has never been here before. She wants to ride the ferris wheel. I do not like the ferris wheel but Katherine does. I will stay on the ground and watch. The line for it is not too long. We go there first. They get on soon and belt themselves in. A man comes over and checks to make sure the bar is latched before their car crosses the threshold on its orbit. They are high in the sky when the wheel stops to let someone else on. They swing back and forth. I am so glad to be on the ground. I shield my eyes trying to look up at them. My hat falls behind the bench. I reach for it. I hear a familiar voice. "I'll get it." It is the boy from the race. "I'm glad you are all right. I wondered if you would be here. My uncle's a cop. He never said your name. I knew it had to be you. Well, I've got to go back to my friends. Be careful." And just as quickly, he was gone, dropping my hat on the bench beside me. Lourdes and Katherine are getting off the ferris wheel. "Yeah, we saw all that that," they say in unison. I shake my head at them, my face turns red, a tear rolls down my cheek. "Hey, wait, what is wrong? We didn't mean anything." They are looking at me, puzzled and concerned. I explain quickly, with as few words and as little emotion as possible. "Momma and I had trouble last night. Someone tried to break in to hurt us. I had to call the police. The boy heard about it from his uncle. We had to stay someplace else. That's why I was late. I can't say anything else right now." My friends understand. "Everything will be OK, everything will be OK," they say. They tell me about everything they could see from the top of the ferris wheel. We eat some of the snacks Ms. Sanders gave me. Wait. There is something else in the backpack. Either Momma or Ms. Sanders has given me a single use camera. I waste no time unwrapping it. We stop one of the teachers as they walk by. We sit on the bench and they take our picture. We ride the old roller coaster and the new one, the ride that tilts and whirls at high speed. The log ride where we all get sprayed with cold water and the giant bouncer. We drink lemonade and eat cotton candy and lacey fried pastry coated with powdered sugar. We dress in old fashioned clothes and have our pictures made. We stop to eat lunch—barbecue for me, corndogs for Katherine and Lourdes, then ice cream. We go through the petting zoo and hold and pet miniature bunnies. I cuddle all of the kittens. Finally, we come to the carousel with its beautiful handpainted, hand carved horses and dragons, camels and swans. Little seated animals for children too small or too scared to ride the others. I make sure we all get a horse or other creature that moves up and down. I take their pictures and they take mine. The carousel is over a hundred years old. Miss Bessie probably rode these same animals as a child. I know she is in her eighties. We ride the carousel twice. I make sure I have a picture of it when it is still, as well as when it is moving. Miss Bessie will want to see it. I ask my friends to pick one more thing to ride or to see. Then we will have to head back to the bus. We head to the crafts building and look at all of the things that people have made; we talk to the man building the rockers. We each try out a rocker. I get his business card. I would love to have a rocker for my room. Lourdes and Katherine and I try out a double rocker; we all squeeze into it, laughing and giggling. The man says we should all buy one of them for our porches for the three of us to rock together at our homes. Katherine tells the man she doesn't have a real porch because she lives in an apartment. He says, if she had one at her apartment, they would probably have to chain it. She agrees. We thank him for his time and showing us how he makes the rockers. We have just enough time to get back to the bus. We run back.

Our teacher marks us off and tells us thank you for being responsible for getting back on time. Some of the others are going to be late. We did not spend all of our money either. I can buy a soft drink this weekend, or if I use all of my money, some new cray-pas or colored pencils from the art store. I just love going in there to look. One day I'm going to have an easel and canvas and oil paints. Momma used to paint. She showed me how to stretch a real canvas. I come back to the present. Everyone is on the bus. We head back to the school.

In the room, the teacher makes sure we are all there and have our things. She tells us that she enjoyed being our teacher and to have a good, safe summer. Then she tells us goodbye. The bell rings. Another year is done. I give my teacher the card that I made her and give her a hug. My friends are waiting. I know where Lourdes lives and where Katherine lives. I will see them this summer. Now I have to go find Ms. Sanders. I don't have to look for long; she is standing off to the side. Other students are crowding around. Then I see why. She has my Teacup with her. Teacup hears, smells me coming and is pulling on her leash. I bend down to greet her and get doggie kisses. "Thank you for bringing Teacup, Ms. Sanders. I hope she wasn't any trouble." "Oh, Child, Jasper and I have had so much fun with this little dog. She wanted to come. Somehow, she knew I was coming to get you. We haven't had a little dog in the house in awhile. Miss Bessie always gets dogs in twos so that they have company. We had two little dogs before we had Jasper and Juno. Little dogs usually live longer."

We get into the car and buckle up. Teacup sits in my lap. I decide to ask Ms. Sanders about the white feather. Ms. Sanders, last night there were two large, white dogs. But when the police came, there was only Jasper. Even the men attacking us saw two dogs and Jasper attacked the man in the field. The other dog got the man at the door. This morning, Teacup found a feather in the foyer and she was wagging her tail. Have you ever found feathers in the foyer?"

Ms. Sanders looked at me. "Child, I find white feathers in the foyer, on the dogbed, in Miss Bessie's room. I find white feathers everywhere. I think God must be letting us know that Juno is OK. God sent you Juno as an angel dog last night. He knew Jasper needed help. I get chills just thinking about it. Talking this way is like going to church. God is so close. If your feather is like the others, it is real soft and white. Not like any feathers I ever seen before."

"I'm glad you don't think I'm crazy. I was sure that Juno was an angel dog, too. I didn't realize it at first. I want to see if there are any white feathers at the garden shed. We left my bicycle there, too."

"Miss Bessie and Jasper are both at the house. She is anxious to talk to you."

"I already know who she is. She always speaks to me at church."

We pull into the driveway. Teacup and I walk back to shut the gates. Ms. Sanders unlocks the front door.

Miss Bessie is in the front parlor with Jasper. In some one else's house it would be a living room, but in this house it is a front parlor. Jasper gets up to greet me, wagging his tail. He is limping and his left front leg is bandaged. Miss Bessie says he was grazed by a bullet. Those men did have a gun. Miss Bessie tells me to put my things away and get a snack. I also take the leash off of Teacup. She is already playing with Jasper.

The babies are sleeping in the youth bed. I get a sandwich and some lemonade. Miss Bessie says that she will come into the kitchen. Jasper and Teacup stay in the parlor to play. Miss Bessie sits down at the far end of the table. I move to the seat on her left, so Ms. Sanders can sit across from me on the right. I say my blessing and wait for Miss Bessie to begin talking. I offer to make her a sandwich. She declines. Ms. Sanders gets her some coffee. She puts cream in it. The wonderful rich smell of coffee fills the kitchen.

"So, where to begin?" Miss Bessie asks. "Do you feel like talking now? You do not have to tell us everything. I know a lot has happened. I do believe that God has brought us together and that He sent Juno and Jasper to you. Juno has been gone about a year. In fact, it was a year yesterday. How did you ever know my address? You have never been here."

"Your address was in an old church directory, in the shed, with the old hymnals and your rocks and the rusty rat traps..." My voice trails off. "We have been living there about a year. Your fly rod and your picture were there, too. I didn't connect everything and realize it was you, until last night when the man said he had "whacked you" and shot Jasper." I knew the police would not know that something had happened to you. I wanted them to make sure that you were all right. I'm sorry the police took one of your

59

rocks. They said it was evidence because I smashed the man's hand with it. I have the other rocks. I brought them and the picture to you, and the fly rod. I knew you wouldn't want the rat traps. Having your picture gave me someone to talk to sometimes. I imagined what you were like when you were my age." I am crying again.

Miss Bessie pats my arm. "We did not mean to upset you. I am thrilled that you found my rocks. I have searched for them for years. I collected rocks when I was younger. I can't wait to see them."

I go get the rocks and the picture and Miss Bessie's fly rod. She beams when I put them in her hands.

"Child, we have bothered you enough. Go take a nap. If the babies wake, we will get them. Take Teacup, too. Jasper needs to nap."

Jasper is trying to nap. Teacup wags all over when she sees me. Jasper has been letting her win. The ends of his ears are damp where she has chewed them. She tumbles over him one more time. I scoop her up and head for the bedroom. I get undressed and crawl gratefully into the bed with Teacup in my arms. I pet her and let her move to the other side of the bed. The bed feels so good.

I awaken an hour later. At first I am scared. I don't know where I am. It is afternoon, but I am not at the cousin's house. The babies, where are the babies? I throw on my clothes. Teacup jumps off the bed. Wait, wait. We are safe, we are at Miss Bessie's. I lay back down for a minute. I put T back on the bed. She climbs on top of me and lays her head on my shoulder as she nuzzles my ear. I breathe deeply, relax and pet her for a little while longer. "T, we have to get up." She looks at me. We get up and I put on my shoes. She probably needs to go out. Jasper is still in the parlor in the sunlight. He wants to go out, too. I sit on the porch and watch them run around the yard, mentally marking where I need to clean up. The sunlight feels good. Ms. Sanders comes out. "Miss Bessie is sleeping. She was like a child at Christmas with these things that you brought her. And Jasper has had such a good time with Teacup. Do you drink coffee, yet? I just made a new pot."

Coffee. A sunny afternoon, good company, good dogs and coffee.

It would be perfect if Momma and Daddy were here. Ms. Sanders has the babies in the kitchen. I get the backpacks and show her how to put my brother in his and put it on. I put Em in her backpack. We get our coffee and go back outside on the porch. Em pats my back. "Momma," she says. "Momma." My brother is looking for Momma. Suddenly, the dogs are barking. Jasper and T both run to the fence. It is Momma! She is walking and smiling, she waves. Em is waving both of her little hands. My brother is bouncing up and down with excitement.

Momma comes in the gate and hugs me. "What a greeting! And do I smell fresh coffee?" Momma is carrying a package. "I thought we needed a treat after last night. I made an extra peanut butter cake."

Ms. Sanders claps her hands. "Miss Bessie will be so happy. She's been hearing about that cake and wanting to try it. I don't believe I've ever had any either. Do we have to wait until after dinner? It would go real good with this coffee. I know Miss Bessie would like it."

As if on cue, Miss Bessie appeared. "Here you all are, gathered on the porch in the sunshine, having fresh coffee and discussing cake, even the dogs are here. Where is this cake?"

We laughed and found Miss Bessie a seat. Jasper came to greet her. Momma set the cake on the table. "I'll go get plates and silverware."

Ms. Sanders was getting Miss Bessie some coffee. I took the plates and forks from Momma and arranged them with the napkins by the cake. Momma carefully unwraps the cake. The aroma fills the air in the breeze. The dogs take notice, putting up their noses and sniffing. T looks at Jasper and they head to the porch. Jasper lays down at a respectable distance from the table and T follows his lead, stretching out against him. She looks like an ink blot up against his large white form.

Momma hands the knife to Ms. Sanders and she cuts Miss Bessie a piece. Momma is waiting to see if Miss Bessie likes it. Miss Bessie looks at it first. "It has a wonderful, permeating aroma. The texture is moist, yet firm. The icing reminds me of fudge. Definitely time to taste and eat." She takes a bite. "Oh, this is wonderful. I was sorry that I was too late to buy this cake at the first bake sale." Momma says thank you. Now we all get to eat. Em and my brother start to fuss. Momma gives each of them a bite. She doesn't want to spoil their dinner. I finish the last of my cake and coffee. I feel so relaxed and safe here, even though it is not our house.

As we clean up, Miss Bessie spots a police car slowing down. "Wait, Ms. Sanders, it looks like we are going to have company. We should offer them some cake and coffee." Ms. Sanders and Momma go to get more plates. I just watch. They are stopping. I put the dogs in the house and go to open the gate. They drive in and up the driveway. Miss Bessie is offering them cake and coffee as I come up on the porch.

"Hello, young lady. We just came to check on you and your family. We get enough information from those two who came to your house. We just haven't figured out where that other dog went to or came from. The man at the door definitely has dog bite wounds. Jasper was sitting on the other man. From what they have said, the other dog looked just like Juno. Anyway, the case is pretty solid. We have the gun and we've been able to tie them to some other crimes. It appears they have been targeting women, Hispanics and anybody they thought they could take advantage of."

They are eyeing the cake. Miss Bessie offers them cake and coffee again. "You won't find any better cake than this and the coffee's fresh." They sit down. One of the officers says, "I know this cake. Someone brought one to the station, said it came from that family restaurant.

"Momma makes it. It is one of her talents, one of her gifts. She just started working at that restaurant," I say.

The officer asks if I have ever heard the men talk about any other crimes- either doing them or planning them. Momma puts her arm around me and Em as she looks at me. I drop my head. "The only other thing they've ever to said to me was about how they wanted to do sexual things to me. They did mention... they did mention a young woman who's Hispanic." I have to stop. All of a sudden I know who they were talking about. "They were talking, planning to hurt Lourdes and her older sister! But when I first heard it, I did not know Lourdes, but now I do! You can't let these men out! You have to keep Lourdes and her sister safe!" I am crying again. I am tired of crying. I want everything to be all right.

Momma holds me as I tell the officers the details that I remember. They will check with Lourdes and her older sister to make sure they are safe.

They thank us for the cake and coffee. They promise to come to the restaurant.

Momma and I are still supposed to go look at the little house. I want to see it. Momma calls Ms. Jackson, our HOW. She is going to come and follow us there. We are going to take Em and my brother, too. Ms. Sanders offers to watch them, but she and Miss Bessie have done enough already and been terribly kind to us. Momma and I make sure we have extra diapers and wipes in the baby bag. Ms. Jackson comes in to meet Ms. Sanders and Miss Bessie. She also has to pet Jasper and T. The dogs really like her. Momma and I will help Ms. Sanders finish dinner when we get back. Momma is going to buy pizzas and we are going to make salads. Of course, we will have more cake for dessert.

We pile into Miss Bessie's car, strap in the babies, strap us in and go. Lourdes and her Mother are waiting on the front porch when we get there. I have been down this street but not really noticed this house before. It is smaller than our first house and certainly smaller than Miss Bessie's. Momma checks out the kitchen while Lourdes shows me the bedrooms. I want the bedroom at the back of the house that has a door to the backyard from the laundry room and lots of windows. Momma likes the large bedroom at the front that is off the living room and has French doors. There is a bedroom in between for the babies. There is an attic and permanent stairs to the attic from the kitchen. There is a doorway from my room to the laundry room and then to the kitchen. The backyard and the front yard are fenced. There is a garden shed in the backyard and two plum trees. There is a tree that I don't recognize that has beautiful tiny pink blooms and really soft leaves. I like this house. Momma likes this house. We can afford it. Momma and Lourdes' Mother talk, working out the details. Em seems to like the house, too. My brother is happy about all of the walking around. Ms. Jackson gives Lourdes' Mother the papers from the agency. I cannot believe how well this has worked out. Momma will have to wait until Monday to pay the utility deposit. Ms. Jackson explains how the agency she works for will pay the first month's rent. Momma signs the lease and gives Lourdes' Mother the deposit. We will not have

63

utilities changed to Momma's name until Monday but we can move our stuff in. Lourdes' Father has a truck and several brothers with trucks. They are going to help us move our things from storage to the house. Momma will take off work and do that tomorrow. I will stay at Miss Bessie's and watch Em and my brother. Our worker, Ms. Jackson, is pleased about the house.

We have a house, a place to live, with doors and windows and a bathroom and everything. The tub is the old kind with claw feet, like at Miss Bessie's. It's large and has a slanted back, so you can lay back and relax. I can't wait to tell Miss Bessie and Ms. Sanders about the house. Momma and I talk about the house on the way back to Miss Bessie's. Momma likes the French doors in her bedroom that open to the living room. There is another set from the living room to the dining room. Her closet is small but Momma has an oak English armoire or wardrobe. It was enough for her and Daddy. Thoughts about Daddy again, think about it just for a minute. I hope Daddy has our letter and papers by now and knows where we are. But now we're moving again! What if Daddy loses us again? Momma reads my thoughts. "The army has the restaurant address, Sweetie, and our bank account number. We are not lost. Now, have you left anything at the cousins' house, other than your plastic storage container, that I need to get tomorrow? If it's small stuff, we can get it now."

Go to the cousins' house where the plan was hatched to rob us, go there? My mind is racing. OK, Momma is with me. I can do this.

"Momma, I can go because you are with me. I do need to just go look and see what is there. Even though it was just yesterday, it seems so long ago, so far away, almost like a different lifetime of somebody else's."

Momma turns towards the cousins' house. We pull up in front of the house and get the babies out, put them in their backpacks. It is comforting to feel Em's little body against mine. We go to the front door and Momma rings the doorbell. Someone actually comes and answers the door. They are surprised to see us but let us in. "That sure is a nice car you got." Momma thanks her for letting us in. Momma agrees about the car and explains why we are here. "You're not taking the rest of the groceries, are you? So I guess that means you're not going to cook for us anymore? What about the utility bill, who's going to pay that now? Momma is so patient and kind, soothing over the woman's anger like lotion on dry skin or ice water on a hot day or calamine on a sunburn. Momma explains that we are leaving the groceries, she will not be cooking for them and we did pay the utility bill. The new bill will not be our responsibility. "The babies will also be going somewhere else. I know some of their things are here. We'll get everything together and get it out of here, out of your way. I know it has been hard on you at times, that we were here." This seems to satisfy the woman somewhat, to appease her anger. We go to the backroom. Momma gathers all the small baby things and puts them in the plastic container. I search under the furniture for stray toys. Momma takes the sheets and blankets from the two twin beds and throws them in, too. The cribs are ours.

"How energetic do you feel? Do you feel like helping me take down these baby beds? They will fit in the trunk."

I am always surprised by Momma's level of energy. How does she do it?

"OK, Mom, I can help do this. Let's get it out of the way." We remove the mattresses and the springs. They are heavier than I thought. Momma shows me how the rods help hold everything together. Finally, she unscrews the wing nuts and puts them in her pocket. So in reality, what really makes the bed sturdy is the interconnectedness and the springs and the mattress. We lean the pieces against the wall and start on Em's bed. It is easier now that I know what I am doing. We begin to carry the pieces out. Momma takes the side pieces, then the mattresses. I carry the end pieces and the springs. After several trips, the beds are loaded. It all fits in the trunk and we tie it down. I help Momma carry out the plastic tub and put it in the back seat. Momma tells the cousins goodbye while I put Em in her car seat. I hear them say that they will miss us. They will miss our groceries, Momma's cooking and Momma paying for things. I do not really think that they will miss us. Momma is so kind. She hugs the woman and tells her goodbye. Momma never said a word about last night.

Momma puts my brother in his car seat and we are ready to go. We drive back to the new house; Momma unloads the baby beds and puts them in the front room. I help her unload the plastic tub. She slides it across the porch, into the house. She makes sure the door is locked. Pizza time. We have a lot to celebrate.

At the pizza place, Momma asks if I want to go in and get our pizzas. Sometimes I feel shy at fast food restaurants and don't want to be the one to go in. But today is OK. I take the money and make sure of what our order is. Em is getting ready to cry. She knows I am getting out of the car without her. I give her a kiss.

Even outside, there is the wonderful aroma of pizza. We are getting a pepperoni with extra cheese and extra large specialty pizza with everything on it, except anchovies. No one wants anchovies, except maybe cats. Now that we are going to have a house, maybe I can have a rescue cat or kitten.

I tell the man our order. He puts two hot pizza boxes on the counter. I open them to make sure they are all right, just like Momma does. I close the boxes, sealing in the wonderful aroma of our dinner. I pay the man and get the change. Em is bouncing up and down in her car seat as I reach for the back door handle.

Momma is enjoying the smell of our pizzas as I buckle in. "Open the box," she says, "just once. I open the box. Even the babies notice the pungent aroma. Close the box. We will soon be at Miss Bessie's. I open the gate; Momma drives in and I shut it. Ms. Sanders, Jasper and Teacup, have come out to greet us. Ms. Sanders takes the pizzas. Teacup scrambles into the car and kisses Em before I can get her unbuckled; she squeals in delight. Momma has my brother. We will get the car seats and baby backpacks later. Jasper and Teacup escort us into the house. I put Em in her highchair and go wash my hands. Momma is finishing the salads so I set the table, making sure everyone has a knife. Sippy cups and napkins, we are done. Ms. Sanders has made tea. We will have coffee after dinner. Ms. Sanders puts the pizzas on a cart by the table. I will be the designated pizza cutter. We sit down and have the blessing; I add my own in my head.

I cut the babies' pieces first so they will cool off. Miss Bessie says that it has been a long time since they had pizza and that perhaps they should have it more often. Ms. Sanders agrees. I serve Miss Bessie and Ms. Sanders next, then Momma and finally me. Ms. Sanders only wants two pieces of speciality pizza. Ms. Bessie, Momma and I each get a slice of pepperoni and a slice of speciality piece pizza. The babies are getting impatient and banging the trays of their highchairs. I quickly cut their pizza into small pieces and place it on their trays. My brother wastes no time in eating his. Em looks as though she has never had pizza before. She picks up a piece in each hand. She sniffs it. She sticks her tongue out and licks the cheese. She smiles and crams it into her mouth. She chews forever, then eats another piece. I just have to make sure I cut hers into really small pieces. My brother wants more. Momma offers to cut pizza for him so that I can eat.

It tastes so good. Whenever we had pizza at the cousins', Momma always had to be the one to buy it. I never got to take leftovers home, even when we had some. I have really enjoyed this time with Miss Bessie and Ms. Sanders. Em has probably eaten most of a slice; my brother has eaten a slice and a half, not counting the part he dropped on the floor. I don't know if I'll have room for dessert. I do eat my salad. We tell Miss Bessie and Ms. Sanders about the house and answer their questions.

After dinner, I help Ms. Sanders with the dishes, while

Momma cleans up the babies. They will go to bed soon. We all gather in the living room. I read to my little brother while Em sits in my lap with him. I talk about the pictures, point out words to him, sound out words and try to get him to answer questions. Em sometimes seems more interested than he does. She points to the book when I do, looks at me and trys to say the words I say. Now that we are going to have our own address again, they can start getting books from the Imagination Library. They send a book a month to children from birth to age five for free. I would like to have some new books to read to them. They are getting sleepy. My brother snuggles closer and shuts his eyes. Em pats him. Momma takes Em so that I can get up from the floor with my brother. They were already in their pajamas. I make sure my brother's diaper is still clean. I get his bear and put him in the bed. Momma puts Em on the other side with her lamb. Em holds it up, looks at us and says, "Lamb." Then she holds it close and goes to sleep. Momma and I kiss them, pull the blanket around them and tiptoe out. T looks at us a moment and follows us out. She lays down against Jasper, looks at him and thumps her tail. He raises his head and licks all of her fur the wrong way.

Miss Bessie asks if there is anything I would like to do. I look at Momma. We have not watched television in a long, long time. I haven't seen one at Miss Bessie's. I know a show that I think comes on that I would like to see. So I explain all this to Miss Bessie. She smiles. "There is a show I like that comes on and I think it's the one you described. I also like some of the crime show investigations, but not the ones that are so graphic. I do have a television; it is in that cabinet over there." Ms. Sanders opens the doors on the cabinet and slides them back. I had only seen those on television or in the furniture store. I like the idea of hiding the television. Momma likes it, too. It would have less baby prints on the screen.

We watch the first program and talk about it during the commercials. The second program is a crime scene investigation

68

show but it is the one that Momma and I liked. I don't know how old Miss Bessie is but she is not how I thought people her age are. Miss Bessie, Momma and Ms. Sanders are going to stay up to watch the news and talk. I am going to walk outside with Jasper and T before I go to bed. I leave the porch light off so that I can see the stars. The moon is out. I sit on the steps while the dogs run through the yard. Other places in the world, people are looking at the stars. I feel peaceful, peaceful and tired. T and Jasper are running along the fence, barking. I do not see anything. They stand at the corner of the yard, T actually up under Jasper. What a picture that would make. They tire of patrolling the perimeter of the yard and join me on the steps, one on each side. For awhile, all I do is pet them and talk to them, stroking their backs, fingering T's silky ears. Then I tell them about the stars. I tell them about the dog star. Jasper is the biggest dog that I have ever been around. My Dad used to sit with me on the steps and look at the stars. Somewhere in storage is a large map of the constellations that used to hang on my ceiling. I remember most of them. T is going to sleep. I rub her back and she opens her eyes. We go back inside. T follows me in as I head through the living room and say goodnight to Miss Bessie and Ms. Sanders; I kiss Momma. I pat Jasper one more time and kiss his big head. Em and my brother are asleep. Once again I get to sleep in this wonderful bed with the ceiling fan whirring overhead and the fluffy pillows. Teacup is whining, she thinks I have forgotten about her. I scoop her up, my face against her and let her lick my face. Then we get into bed. Teacup crawls up close for a few more pets and cuddling. She actually yawns a big puppy yawn right in my face. I barely hear Momma come in. Teacup wakes up long enough to make sure it is Momma. I sleep. Blissful, safe, uninterrupted sleep.

Morning. T is stretched out beside me. Mamma is gone. Miraculously, the babies are still asleep. I get dressed and take Teacup out, Jasper comes, too. I clean up after them and head back to the house, dogs running behind me. I hear Em talking as we go back in. She is kicking off the covers and about to get into mischief by waking my brother. I pick her up, change her and get her some clean clothes. Just as I finish, my brother wakes up. Ms. Sanders comes to the rescue and offers to take Em. I pass Em to Ms. Sanders and reach for my brother. Once he realizes he is not alone, he is happy. I tickle him and talk to him as I change him and get him dressed. I stand him up so that he can walk. He cruises along the edge of the bed. Teacup is carefully watching him. He gets close to her, points and says, "Doggie!"

"Yes, that is a doggie. That is a little, black doggie; her name is Teacup." T moves closer; my brother reaches out to pet her.

"Gentle, gentle. Soft pats." He does pretty well. Teacup wags her tail at him.

He claps his hands and says "Doggie, doggie, doggie."

Em is already in her highchair in the kitchen. I put my brother in his. He looks at Em. He points to T.

"Doggie, doggie." Em smiles. She points to T. She does not try to say the word but she knows what he said. I point to Jasper and say "Doggie. Big, white doggie." They both look at me. I hope they make the generalization.

Breakfast is messy - sausage, little half dollar size pancakes and applesauce. My brother is getting pretty good at feeding himself. Em is still torn between eating and playing. She always seems so excited about food! I wonder if she went hungry before. Ms. Sanders makes sure Em gets enough to eat while I focus on my brother.

After breakfast, after they are cleaned up, we go into the living room and put them on the floor with toys to play. I get them to stack blocks, to sort and match objects and to dump them out. We roll a soft ball. I sound out words for them, emphasizing beginning letters and talking about what they are doing, just like Momma has shown me. Ms. Sanders says that I would be a good teacher. I thank her but let her know that I intend to be a veterinarian and that I hope to work with large animals as well as with dogs and cats. It would be great to work at a zoo, too, or a place that worked with endangered species.

The babies want a change of activities. We make sure they are clean, they have drinks and crackers, wipes and diapers. We decide to use backpacks instead of the strollers. Ms. Sanders knows where there is a park with good swings. Ms. Sanders goes to check on Miss Bessie and let her know that we are leaving. Teacup and Jasper will stay with Miss Bessie. Teacup begins to cry when we start to leave without her. I pick her up and tell her how much I love her and what a good dog she is, that she has to stay to help protect Miss Bessie. Miss Bessie smiles and holds out her arms to take Teacup. T is surprised and licks Miss Bessie in the face. Jasper moves to Miss Bessie's side and wags his tail. We move out the door and Miss Bessie locks it.

It is warm but not too hot just yet. Ms. Sanders has Em because Em is lighter. We talk about school, the weather and Miss Bessie's beautiful house. The house was built after the first house burned when Miss Bessie was about my age. Miss Bessie's Mother and her baby brother died that same winter from the flu. Folks said her Father was never the same after that. After the house burned, he couldn't bear to rebuild it in the same place. People said there was just too much sorrow there so he moved Miss Bessie and her sister to this lot and built a new house. Her sister died two years later. That left only Miss Bessie and her Father.

"Where was the old house?" I ask.

"Child, the old house was back of the church. Miss Bessie had a playhouse she and her sister played in. Later, they used it as a garden shed."

Our garden shed, Miss Bessie's playhouse/garden shed.

"Miss Bessie never married. She looked after her Father and at times, other relatives lived with them. She looked after her younger cousins. She went to college, she trained to be a lawyer. No one would hire her. She worked for her Father as the company lawyer. He was in the cotton business. They made it through the Depression and helped others to make it, too. That was before he had his children, before her time. When her Father died, she ran the cotton business, training her cousins in the business. When she retired, she taught school at her home, girls only. After that, she busied herself with charity work and her hobbies. She traveled a good bit. She reads everything, knows Latin, Greek and French. Taught herself Spanish. There were many men who wanted to marry her but she would not marry. She felt it would compromise her as a person, that no man would allow her to be herself."

I cannot believe my fortune in knowing someone like Miss Bessie.

We are at the park. There are tall, old fashioned swings for people like me as well as a section for smaller children. I am going to swing first, before I take my brother out of his back. pack. I have Ms. Sanders check to make sure he is secure. I start out slowly, to make sure he is OK with it. Ms. Sanders says he is smiling. Then I swing higher. He is laughing out loud. I do not swing as high as I want or as high as I can. I can do that later when my brother is not with me. I go back and forth a few more times, then gradually slow down. Now, Ms. Sanders will swing with Em. I can tell that Em is impatient and does not want to wait. I make sure Em is secure. Ms. Sanders laughs, "I am not going to go as high as you did. Em may feel that she has been cheated."

Em's eyes get big as Ms. Sanders starts off. She likes the wind in her face. She is smiling. She holds onto the backpack. Ms. Sanders goes a little higher for a few more times and stops. "I had forgotten how much exercise this is, especially with the extra weight." Em had a good time, she does not appear to be disappointed about anything. I got several good pictures.

We go to the slides next. I take my brother out of his backpack. He can climb the steps with a little help. I make sure he doesn't fall. He gets to the top and I help him hold on while he sits down. He looks toward the end of the slide. He looks at me. I go to the end of the slide. "Come on, slide down. Come to me, you can do it."

At first he is scared, but then he looks at me and lets go of the handles. He loses his balance at first, regains it and comes flying down the slide. "More, more, more." Ms. Sanders is taking pictures. I lift him down and walk him back to the steps. Em is curious. Ms. Sanders puts her at the top of the slide and slides her down. Em smiles. I take my brother up and down the slide about 5 more times. Em goes down one last time. There is a sandbox but we decide that is not for today. There are some little spring horses that rock back and forth. I show my brother the horses. "Doggie," he says. "Doggie, doggie." I gently correct him. "Horsie, this is a horse. Three horsies, red, blue and black." He looks at me, his hazel eyes sparkling. He was listening. "Orsie?" "Yes." I emphasize the h sound for him again. "A horsie has four legs like a dog, but it runs faster than a dog and is much bigger." He smiles and I pick him up, placing him on the horse and strapping him in. He is holding on to the handles; I show him how to move it and let him go on his own; he is fine. I wish Momma was here to see this. Ms. Sanders puts Em on a horse and buckles the safety harness; then slowly rocks it. We will have to get them a rocking horse or two. Ms. Sanders and I repeat the words "horsie" and "rocking." We have been gone way longer than we planned; we need to head back to the house. We give Em and my brother juice before we start back.

"Backpacking these babies will really get you in shape. Maybe we could hook up a cart and let Jasper pull them," Mrs. Sanders says.

I laugh. "The babies would like that, but Teacup would want to ride, too."

Ms. Sanders continues. "There used to be a large pedal car in the garage and the two 3 wheeled bicycles. We took turns pedaling

"I would love to see them. I would be happy to pedal Miss Bessie around the neighborhood," I reply.

"As I recall, two, maybe more people could pedal. Of course, only one person could steer. I would help you pedal, Child. I would like to ride in it again."

"Do you think that we could look for them after lunch while the babies sleep?"

"I don't see why not. They are going to be dusty, maybe have some rust on them. But today would be good day to do it."

I cannot wait. It will be like searching for treasure. The dogs are out front and Miss Bessie is on the porch. "The dogs have had a good time, playing and running the yard, while we waited. That little Teacup thinks she is a big dog, just like Jasper."

"Hi, Miss Bessie. The babies had a good time at the park. They are tired. Ms. Sanders said backpacking babies is a workout. I guess I am just used to it. I'm going to go help Ms. Sanders with lunch."

Ms. Sanders and I go into the house. We put Em and my brother in their high chairs and clean their hands and faces. Ms. Sanders gives them some green beans to eat by themselves while we get lunch ready. There is chicken salad with apples, grapes and pecan bits in it. Ms. Sanders says Miss Bessie made it. There is also fresh fruit. I set out bread and croissants with Romaine lettuce and tomatoes, mayonnaise. There is tea and lemonade to drink.

"You do such a nice job of setting the table, dear. Your Mother has taught you well."

"Thank you, Ms. Sanders. Is Momme coming for lunch, too?"

"I don't know. Miss Bessie may have heard from her. Go see."

Miss Bessie is still sitting out front, petting the dogs. "Have you come to summon us to lunch?"

"No, ma'am. I just came to see if you had heard from Momma. Do you think she is coming for lunch?"

"Well, I don't think that she has called. If they want to get everything done today, they will need to move quickly. They are probably eating as quickly as possible."

She must have noticed my face.

"Don't fret. I'm sure she is all right. The police are keeping an eye out for you. I know an old lady and her housekeeper/companion are not the best company for you but we are glad to have you with us. Jasper is just beside himself with adoration for Teacup."

"Miss Bessie, you are not bad company. You and Ms. Sanders and Jasper are wonderful. You took us in; I've had a soft, comfy bed with feather pillows and a ceiling fan. You've been kind and generous. You haven't asked us for money. Even our own relatives always ask for money. Momma always cooked dinner for them and paid them to look after Em and my brother."

"Child, child. You and your family are a gift to us. Give me a hug and let's go eat lunch."

It feels good to get another hug. Most of my hugs come from Momma and the babies.

I and Jasper follow us into the cool air of the house. Em and my brother are happily banging the trays of their highchairs. I give them some macaroni and cheese. No one has ever said we were a gift to them. That is the kind of thing Momma would say to someone.

Miss Bessie says the blessing. I am going to eat a croissant sandwich, maybe two. It is so wonderful to have fresh lettuce and tomatoes, just sitting in the refrigerator, waiting. The new house has a refrigerator. I keep an eye on Em and my brother while I fix my ~~sandwidge~~ sandwich. I'm going to eat rye bread for the second one.

"I expect you'll be needing to eat more than one sandwich. We have plenty. We've saved the pizza for you to take to your new house tomorrow."

"Thank you, Miss Bessie. You're right. I may eat a second sandwich or half of one."

The babies are looking at me. I give them strawberry pieces. I finish the first sandwich. I am going to wait a few minutes and see if I feel full. Ms. Sanders begins asking Miss Bessie about the pedal car and the bicycles. "You remember the pedal car and the bicycles that we used to ride short distances in good weather? Aren't they still in the garage?"

Miss Bessie waits before answering. "Well now, I don't know. I don't remember giving them away and I know that I didn't sell them. They ought to be out there - certainly dusty and maybe with some rust."

I laugh. "That is exactly what Ms. Sanders said. 'Do you care if I look for them while the babies nap?'"

"No, no. You look for them. We'll find them and if they are working, we'll take a ride. It's a good day for a ride, give the neighbors something to talk about."

Ms. Sanders smiles and shakes her head. "People will always talk. You do the right thing - they talk. You do the wrong thing - they really talk. They've been talking about this house and what goes on, for a long time."

I eat another half sandwich. I give Em and my brother their sippy cups. They've had enough to eat, too. Jasper and I are eating stray bits of macaroni and cheese. I finish my sandwich as the babies finish their sippy cups; I manage to get the cups before they drop them to the floor. Ms. Sanders takes my brother and I take Em - cleanup, diapers, nap.

We head to the garage. There are old garden tools, new garden tools, bicycle parts, garden hose, ladders, carpenter tools. Ms. Sanders goes to the back where there is a series of olive green tarps, thick with dust. "I think this is it. Let's move the tarps. Be careful of the dust," Ms. Sanders warns. We each take an edge of the tarp. These tarps are heavy. We turn our heads to avoid the dust as we set the tarp on the ground. "I had forgotten how beautiful they are," Ms. Sanders exclaims as she runs her hands over the frames.

I have never seen bicycles like these where I could actually touch them. I have only seen them in pictures or advertisements. There is a black bicycle, and a red one. Large seats, large tires, big roomy baskets between the two back tires. Ms. Sanders begins to move the red bicycle out of the garage. I take the black one. They are beautiful. Ms. Sanders heads back into the garage. "The pedal car is here, too. I'll definitely need your help with that." Ms. Sanders takes the cloth we brought to wipe everything down and we go to the very back of the garage. The second tarp is really large. We take the far edge of it and lift to the next edge as though we were folding a bedsheet or quilt. "Try to fold it and then let it down to the ground," Ms. Sanders says. In the dim light, I see the size of the car. It would easily hold 6 people - certainly someone my size with two babies and a dog or two. Put the babies on the second seat in their carriers, I could ride in the front or with the babies. Jasper will need a seat on the back row by himself. I could pedal alone or have help. Ms. Sanders is giving it the once over, sizing up our task. "Let's wipe out the seats; then you and I are going to pedal into the sunlight." She cleans the front seat and the steering wheel; I clean the seat on the other side. We get in. It is totally open on the sides; it does have a solid floor. "Miss Bessie's father had them make the floor solid; it was just steel bars. He wanted it solid for safety reasons. He was a forward thinking person. Not everyone understood him." There are no seat belts. Ms. Sanders looks around to make sure we have a clear path. "Are you ready to pedal? We'll work off our lunch." She turns the steering wheel and we put our feet on the pedals. We push hard at first. These pedals have not been moved in awhile. There is a bit of a squeak. Slowly, we begin to move on the dirt floor. This is amazing. The babies are going to love this. A few turns of the pedals and we are out in the sunlight.

Miss Bessie cheers from the porch. "You found them. I can't wait to ride."

Ms. Sanders stops and we get out; she hands me the cloth. "You start wiping off the dust. I'll go get a bucket of soapy water and some cloths."

I wipe the bicycles first, then the pedal car. Ms. Sanders returns. "I'm going to sit a minute, child. Then we'll make them sparkle."

I sit down, too. Miss Bessie starts to laugh. "Ms. Sanders and I almost get a ticket one time. We were on the bicycles; we had gone to the grocery, the produce market really, and we were headed home. The policeman stopped us, said we were speeding. I knew we weren't. The cars were passing us."

Ms. Sanders takes up the story. "The policeman really just wanted to talk to Miss Bessie. He wanted a date was what he wanted." She winked at me.

"Ms. Sanders, how you do carry on. We did have him over for Sunday dinner, though. I made chocolate cake. The war started shortly after that, that month as I recall. He left and he never came back, sad for his family. He did like that chocolate cake. I think it's very similar to that one your Momma makes. We rode our bicycles and walked and drove that pedal car. They didn't want people using gasoline. Some people thought we should have given up the pedal car for the war effort to recycle metal, but we needed it. We took people to church in it and to the grocery store. It looked real pretty at Easter. All the ladies dressed up. We even put flowers on it."

"I remember. It did look awful pretty with all those flowers on it. I think there's a picture somewhere. You know Mr. Wylund did love his pictures. We get a whole mess of pictures you need to go through and write who it is and the date."

Miss Bessie agreed. "Now let's get these cleaned up while these sweet babies are still asleep and before it gets any hotter. Otherwise, we'll need to be selling lemonade while we drive around."

Ms. Sanders laughed. "And that's another story for another day."

The warm soapy water almost dried on the frames before I could rinse them. Miss Bessie played fetch with the dogs with a ball I had found in the garage. I couldn't quite pick up the ball so she rolled it with her nose to Jasper; then he took it to Miss Bessie. We cleaned the bicycles first. I could either carry both babies in the basket or one baby and I. Miss Bessie says the black bicycle was hers and was the taller of the two because she was always taller. Her Father special ordered it for her. Not many girls had bicycles and certainly not a bicycle as fine as this one. I love the big wide seat and the heavy frame. It even has a horn. I dry the seat and sit down. It feels good. Miss Bessie says we'll have to check the chain. It's not rusty and it's on, not off the gear wheel. The gear wheel has all of its points to catch the chain as it makes around. The spokes within the wheel are all there and tight. Miss Bessie took good care of her bicycle, just like I took good care of my books. The tires are flat but do not have dry rot. Miss Bessie sends me back into the garage for the pump. Ms. Sanders shows me how to attach the hose to the tire and pump up the tire. It is not hard but it is tiring. I do the tires on the black bicycle first, then the red one. After that, I go sit in the shade on the porch and pet the dogs; they are resting, too. I offer to go get Miss Bessie and Ms. Sanders something to drink. Miss Bessie sends me to the big refrigerator in the pantry for soft drinks. I check on the babies and go to the pantry. I wipe off the tops of the cans, get paper towels and straws for Miss Bessie and Ms. Sanders. I love the quiet of this house. There's no arguing, no one yelling about dinner being late, no beer smell.

I bring the drinks out and set them on the table. The dogs look thirsty. I ask Miss Bessie about an outdoor water dish. Ms. Sanders thinks there is one in the garage and helps me look. We find it and I wash it out. Jasper comes running to the hose and T tries to bite the water. I fill the bowl and put it in the shade. T stands between Jasper's legs and drinks water. He doesn't care. I quickly take their picture. Jasper stops and licks the top of T's head, ruffling her fur so it sticks up on the top of her head. I get that picture as well.

Miss Bessie laughs. "Jasper, you always lick Teacup's hair the wrong way and she is such a pretty little dog."

"Teacup doesn't care, Miss Bessie. She loves him," I reply. We all sit in the deep shade of the porch for awhile watching the dogs. Ms. Sanders looks at me. "Are you ready to tackle the pedal car?" I nod affirmatively and we step out into the sunlight.

I stand on the edge of the car and clean half the canopy. Then switch sides and clean the other half. Ms. Sanders washes down the inside. We each inflate a tire, two left. Finally, the last tire is clean and inflated. Miss Bessie comes off the porch and walks around the pedal car, running her hands over the frame. "So many memories." She turns to Ms. Sanders and me, "OK, let's put the dogs on leashes. I'll sit with them in the car. Get these sweet babies. We're going for a ride!"

Ms. Sanders gets the leashes and I head for Em and my brother. I can hear them chattering as I come in the house. "Babies, babies, we are going for a ride. We have to get you ready." I take my brother out of the bed and change him. Ms. Sanders comes in as I finish.

"Go ahead and take him out and buckle him in his car seat. I'll take care of Em."

Em looks like she is going to cry. She thinks she is being left. "Em, Precious," I tell her, "you are not being left." She calms down and I carry my brother outside. Miss Bessie is sitting in the backseat with Jasper and Teacup. She holds her hands out to take my brother. "I'll hold him while you get the car seats," Miss Bessie says, "they should fit on the second seat."

I get the car seats and set them on the grass, tilting them to let the crumbs out. I manage to attach them securely to the seat. Ms. Sanders appears with Em; we buckle them in. They are looking around. They appear to like it but they don't understand. Teacup and Jasper are wagging their tails. "This is just like old times," comments Miss Bessie, "except that now I am part of the old."

"Miss Bessie, you are not old, you are my friend. You and Ms. Sanders, my new friends. It has been a good week for new friends." I take a picture of everyone.

Ms. Sanders and I are settled in our seats. She looks at me. "Are you ready? Our maiden voyage, after all these years, out again in the neighborhood."

"Let's go! I took the picture, we have to go!"

Pedaling out of the yard is hard work, going down the driveway is easier. We stop so I can open and shut the gate.

Ms. Sanders turns to Miss Bessie. "You think we'll be OK on the street? We're almost too big for the sidewalk. We would be like several bicycles.

"Traffic is a lot heavier than it used to be, no horse and buggies. Try the sidewalk first. We've got these babies," Miss Bessie replies.

Ms. Sanders turns right; we are heading towards the park. Ms. Sanders says there is a paved trail there that we can ride on. Miss Bessie agrees, "That paved trail at the park, that would be great. I had forgotten about it."

After awhile, I get used to pedaling in rhythm with Ms. Sanders and I can relax. I bet two people could get this up to 35 mph. Now I can look at the people we pass and wave. Miss Bessie is waving. My brother is laughing; Em is waving some of the time. Teacup is either on the seat or in Miss Bessie's lap. People are smiling as we drive by. "Good to see you out again" or "I see you've got extra help."

I notice Ms. Sanders is using hand signals for turns and stopping. I will have to learn those in case she ever lets me drive. The street we are on is really busy and we are going to have to make a left turn across it to get to the park. All of a sudden, a police car appears. It is the officers who came the night the men came, two days and a lifetime ago. "Miss Bessie, is that you? Well now, this is a fine contraption; I see you get everybody including big old Jasper and that pretty little black puppy. You got two good drivers. We'll have to come by one day and get a ride." Then he looked at me. "OK, we'll also help pedal." I smile, embarrassed. "We'll do our job here and stop traffic."

The other officers gets out and stops traffic, as the first officer turns on the lights on the car. Traffic stops, we make our turn and Miss Bessie waves to everyone. It is almost like being on a parade float. The officers turn, too. "Have a good time. We'll be by after dinner this evening with some new information. Don't pedal too fast, we'd hate to give you a ticket."

"I won't let them get too fast. Ms. Sanders has been making sure that she signals everything. We'll see you tonight. We'll probably still have cake left." Miss Bessie smiles and we drive off.

The path through the park goes by the golf course, past the art college and around by the playground. I did not notice this trail before. We may not be able to go down the whole trail as it is for runners, walkers and bicyclists, and it may become narrower. Momma and I have never been on it. When you are homeless, you don't have to seek out extra opportunities to walk. There are too many times you have to walk, no matter how tired you are. People wave as they pass us. Just ahead of us is a group of runners, but they look younger, maybe my age. There are two adults running with them. Someone looks familiar, it is the boy I raced with, Ben. He looks at us and smiles, then sees me. He moves up and talks to one of the adults. They wave us down.

Ms. Sanders says, "It looks like they want us to stop. There's too many of them for us to give them a ride, but we'll stop." We pull to the side so that we are not blocking the whole path. The boy and the two adults come up to the car.

"Good afternoon, I'm Coach McIntyre and this is Coach Nelson. I believe this is the young lady I've been hearing so much about. Pedaling like this is good training." I try to look at them without being embarrassed. I manage to tell them my name and say hello. "I do like to run. It is the one thing that I have been able to keep doing. Mainly, I do it for me, not anyone else. I almost always end up running by myself."

Pointing to Ben, Coach McIntyre says, "It is my understanding you had the fastest time the school has ever seen and flew past this guy."

"I did beat him. He ran a good race."

Coach McIntyre continues, "I see you are busy now, but here's the card for our group. Have your Mother call me or Coach Nelson if you're interested in training or just want someone to run with."

I tell them thank you and take the card. Miss Bessie wants a card, too. We tell them goodbye and Ms. Sanders pulls back onto the trail. Miss Bessie says we will need to head back home after we circle the lake, she also tells me that Ben is a fine looking young man and she thinks his family is part of the attorney group she knows.

Miss Bessie is right. Ben is different from any of the other boys that I have known. Most of them are just not interested in the things that I am interested in, they seem silly in how then act and many are not serious about their grades. I know that I will probably need a scholarship and their are two other children in our family who will need a higher education as well.

The trail takes us to a different exit but Ms. Sanders knows how to get us back where we started. Several children at the playground want to ride, too, but there is no room. Soon we are back at the beginning of the trail. Miss Bessie asks if we are too tired to swing by the vegetable market.

Ms. Sanders and I look at each other. "I'm tired, but not too tired to make that stop. The babies are happy and the dogs are happy." Ms. Sanders agrees. Teacup is sleeping in Miss Bessie's lap. We turn toward the market. I know how to get there from here. I help Ms. Sanders watch for cars before we make our turns. We pull into the parking lot. It is almost full but there is a space up front. Ms. Sanders sets the brake.

"I will stay with everybody. Here's the money," Miss Bessie says.

I take the money and hand it to Ms. Sanders. Miss Bessie continues, "We need bananas, check the strawberries. If the tomato plants look good, get 2 for large/regular tomatoes and 2 for cherry tomatoes."

I love going in this place; Momma and I went at least once a week when I was younger. Ms. Sanders goes to check out the bananas and strawberries; I head to the discount table. I still have money left over from yesterday. There are 3 tomato plants on the table with broken stems, 2 regular and 1 cherry, all for a $1.00. Momma will be pleased. The rooted part of the plant will put out new leaves and branches from the stem of the original plant. The broken stem can be rooted, so actually, we have the potential of 6 plants for a $1.00. Ms. Sanders has bananas and strawberries. The other plants are in front of the store. We put the bananas and strawberries in a basket while we select tomato plants for Miss Bessie. We find three, one of them is already blooming. Ms. Sanders says, "I wish they'd had six plants that were on the discount table. You were smart; you knew right where to go. In war time, everybody had a garden."

"Plants are pretty resilient; they will come back if you care for them. Actually, people are like that, too."

"We seem to have everything; let's go pay."

Teacup barks a greeting and Jasper thumps his tail. Miss Bessie takes the tomato plants. I put the strawberries and banana up front with the tomato plants that I bought. Now to pedal home. We back up; Miss Bessie helps as a lookout and we are out of the parking lot. I am ready for air conditioning and a nap. Fortunately, the trip home goes faster, as do most return trips; I don't know why that is. I know the distance is the same.

As we get close to the house, Miss Bessie checks for cars behind us, in case we have to be in the street. We stop on the sidewalk and I get out to open the gates. Jasper and I want out, too, but they will have to wait. I hop back in and Ms. Sanders and I make our turn into the driveway. I shut the gates and unleash the dogs, then help Miss Bessie out. Ms. Sanders and I pedal up the walkway to the house; we will wait on going into the garage. We set the plants on the table. Miss Bessie takes the strawberries and bananas into the house. Time for diaper changes, clean hands and snacks. I hope they will let me nap for an hour.

The babies are settled in their highchairs with crackers, cheese pieces and bits of banana. They mush the banana before they eat it. Major yuck! I make sure they each have some cool water, too. I would not want to be a single mom with a couple of kids, certainly not two babies. Pedaling the car with a full load of passengers is hard work. Miss Bessie and Ms. Sanders seem tired, too.

"Dear, I know you haven't had time to think about it, but do you think you might want to run with the church group?" Miss Bessie asks. "That young man sure lit up when he saw you. So he's the one you beat in that race. I sure would have liked to have seen that race."

"Miss Bessie, I've never run with other people. I used to run with my Dad. When... (I have to stop for a minute) when we lost our house, running was all that I had left, except for Momma and my brother, and then Em and Teacup. I don't know if I can share running with anyone. I share my drawings with Momma and sometimes what I write, but I still run just for me. Before, Momma would backpack my brother and ride my bicycle, while I ran. Then she was too tired and we had to live different places. My bicycle was in storage. As long as I had shoes, and it was light still, I could run. I ran after school, on the way to the cousin's house, after I left my friend Katherine, any way I could fit running in. Running kept me strong. I had to stay strong."

Miss Bessie says she understands. "One day, I will tell you about the times I had to stay strong. Because of the times when I grew up, I ran secretly." She smiles.

"Well, there were many times the black and mixed girls had to run, but we are not getting into that." Ms. Sanders shakes her head. I have read about slavery and civil rights struggles, I _know_ what Ms. Sanders means.

The babies are finished with their snacks. Em reaches up to me and I take her from her highchair. My brother is still eating. I clean her hands and face and put her in the youth crib. My brother has finished eating. I take him next. Ms. Sanders says she will clean the trays. My brother pats my face, he points to me. I say my name, he tries to say it. I say it again. Then he smiles at me and says, "Doggie." We both laugh. He has made a joke.

I clean his face and hands. He does pat-a-cake. I give him a kiss and put him next to Em. Teacup has been trailing me. I put her on the bed as I sit down and take off my shoes and socks. I lay my clothes on the other side of the bed and crawl between the sheets. Teacup snuggles against me and lets out a long puppy sigh. We are both going to sleep.

I wake up to Momma next to me. "Hey, Precious. You have a room again. I tried to set everything up the way I thought you wanted it. I heard you had a big day. I saw the tomato plants. I love you."

"I love you, too, Momma. I can't wait to see my room. Are we going there tonight? Are we spending the night there?"

"We will spend the night here. We still have to have groceries and cleaning supplies. I want us to go to church with Miss Bessie. We will get groceries and cleaning supplies after church. But right now, we have two fussy babies."

I rub T's soft silky side and give her a kiss before I roll over and reach for my clothes. My brother is sitting up, calling to Momma. She picks him up first. I put T in the baby bed with Em. Em squeals and reaches for T. T gets quiet and lays down. Em rubs her hands up and down T's fur, sometimes rubbing it the wrong way. T lets her. "Doggie," I say to Em. "Teacup." My brother looks at me, recognizing the word. "Doggie. Doggie, doggie, doggie. Tea-cup. Teacup. Teacup." Teacup wags her tail and moves towards my brother.

"My goodness! All these words today, have you been holding out on me?" Momma asks. My brother giggles as Momma picks him up and heads to the kitchen. Teacup barks to follow as Jasper comes in. I put T down and pick up Em. I pat Jasper as he turns to go.

"Em, Em, Em, when are you going to give us words?" She watches my face as I talk to her, her dark brown eyes reflecting my face.

"Serious, intent child, how was your life before you came to us. She starts making different letter sounds and looking at me. I make the sounds the back to her and talk to her while I change her. I tell her about the new house and her room, about the yard. She listens. I pick her up and carry her into the kitchen. She leans into me, close. The smell of spaghetti wafts through the house. It will be our last night here. Part of me will stay here and remember the safety and stability, the love of Miss Bessie and Ms. Sanders, given to us even though we were strangers, Jasper's willingness to protect and give his life, the endurance and resilience of Miss Bessie and Ms. Sanders, their understanding of going through hard times. Maybe I will be able to come back and visit.

The kitchen is busy - 4 cooks and two babies, two dogs in the hallway; it feels like a special occasion or holiday, when everyone helps with the cooking. The noodles are almost done, the meat is in the sauce bubbling in the skillet - onions, green peppers, garlic and other spices. Momma has done the salads.

"Child, I am going to sit down and entertain these babies since it is my last night with them. Of course, you realize you will have to come back and visit. It has been too long since young folks and a puppy were here. Ms. Sanders and I had a wonderful time today. Would you butter the bread and put it in the oven?"

"I had a good time, too, Miss Bessie. I would love to come back to visit. I was hoping that I could. I'll be glad to fix the bread." Miss Bessie gets up and gives me a hug.

"It has been such a joy to have you with us. You have been just the gift that Ms. Sanders and I needed. I think Ms. Sanders and I will have to start taking that pedal car out on a regular basis so we can get back in shape. I'll have to go buy some athletic shoes so I can pedal better."

Ms. Sanders laughs. "I haven't had a workout like that in a long time. I'm going to be sore tomorrow. I did take a good nap." Turning to Miss Bessie she says, "You know they're going to talk about us now. We start back pedaling that car around. But I like pedaling that car, makes me feel young and like we live in an easier time. We could save on gas."

The babies are banging their trays. I give them each a small bread/cheese stick and slide the loaf in the oven. Miss Bessie says the blessing and we begin loading our plates from the stove. I fix the baby plates. I would really rather feed them spaghetti than to have them feed themselves. Momma reads my mind. "I know, mess. But they need to learn to do it themselves."

I eat my salad while I keep an eye on Em. She is finishing her breadstick. She eyes my salad. I offer her a bite. She takes it and then makes a face. I tell her it is good and make an mmm sound. She chews, moving everything around in her mouth as though she is checking it out with her tongue. She swallows it and then makes a grab for my fork. I give her another bite of salad and then offer a bite of spaghetti. Oh, good, she is going to let me feed her spaghetti. Momma hands me my spaghetti. I get to eat a few bites before I have to feed Em another bite. We continue this way, Em gets a bite, I get two, until I am finished. I feed Em the last of hers and I eat my bread. I'd like to have coffee. Momma says I can. I put the milk in first, so the coffee will stay hot and mix as I pour in the coffee. I sit back down to savor this time, the feeling of family around a dinner table, the strength of women, the short time that children are babies. I am lost in my thoughts.

Momma and Miss Bessie are talking about banana pudding, maybe discussing recipes. Oh wait, we have banana pudding, that is different. Miss Bessie made it. She gets special dessert bowls from the counter. The pudding has vanilla wafers like Momma's and meringue on the top, but Miss Bessie puts sour cream in it with the vanilla pudding mix. Miss Bessie serves everyone, using two small dainty bowls for Em and my brother. The pudding has a richer flavor, I almost feel guilty eating it. Momma is wondering how many calories it adds to use sour cream. There has to be a way to figure that mathematically. I am not going to worry about the calories.

Ms. Sanders laughs. "We can't be eating like this every night. Not unless we are all going to run. You get those new shoes Miss Bessie and then I guess we could at least walk fast."

We are all laughing now, let loose, tears rolling down our cheeks, laughing. I know Miss Bessie and Ms. Sanders have not run in years, decades. It feels good to laugh like that. The babies watch us curiously and then they laugh, too.

I can't give Em her pudding fast enough. My brother finishes his and checks to see if Em has finished hers. I give them each one more bite. Momma says she will watch them after dinner if I help clean them up. It will be great to have a little free time although I do love Em and my brother. I didn't really plan on caring about Em like I do. To be honest, I was actually more excited about Teacup. So much has happened this week. I can't imagine not having Teacup and Em.

Em is looking at me, patting my arm. She knows that I am thinking about other things. I hold my hands out and she reaches for me. I pick her up and play with her springy curls. She has sticky hands. I let her grab my shirt anyway, as I kiss the top of her head. OK, I can't really give Em up either. Teacup and Jasper follow us into the bedroom; they lay down to wait.

Em just has a dirty face and hands. I get her cleaned up and into her pajamas. I grab her favorite toy. We are going to the front yard to wait on the dogs; they are eager to be outside. It is not yet dark. I spot the police car before it gets to the gate. I put the dogs inside and walk down with Em to open the gate. I let them through and close the gate. Miss Bessie and Ms. Sanders have come out on the porch. Em waves at the policeman, then goes shy and hides her face against me. Momma comes out with my brother. Miss Bessie offers them a seat, then coffee and dessert.

"You have a choice tonight, chocolate fudge cake or banana pudding. Think about it a minute, then decide." Ms. Sanders smiles and then leaves for the kitchen. Still carrying Em, I follow her to help. I get the silverware and the cake; Ms. Sanders gets the plates and the pudding. "I'll come back for the coffee. They came to talk to you and your Mother."

We set everything down on the table and I sit down with Em. The officer looks at me and Momma. "Now that we have these two men in custody, they have decided to talk. There are several robberies that were unsolved. We have been able to implicate them and they are providing the details. As a result of that, Crime stoppers has made the decision to award you the money." He says this last statement while looking directly at me. Money, we're going to get money. Now we can start saving for a house. Can't stay with my thoughts too long, have to answer; stay in the conversation and respond.

"Thank you, sir. I never expected a reward. I just knew we had to be safe and I couldn't let those men get to us."

"We know you don't want a lot of publicity. We'd like for

you and your Mother to come to the station tomorrow afternoon to let us present the check to you and have your picture made. By the way, because of the number of crimes that have been solved, they combined the rewards. The cash amount will be $5,000. Now let's get to that dessert."

I just look at him. Miss Bessie and Ms. Sanders are dishing out pudding and pouring coffee. One of the officers is taking a piece of cake with him. Finally, I find my words."

"Sir, are you sure that is all right? That's a lot of money. Maybe there is someone who needs the money more than we do. We do need it, I won't deny that. I really don't know what to say. Thank you. We will be there tomorrow, all of us." Miss Bessie nods her head and confirms it.

I take Em and go sit in the rocker, leaving the adults to talk. $5,000. What do we need to do with it? Part of it has to go to the church or another charity, or they could divide that part. Part of it needs to go to savings... Momma and I will have to talk about this later. The officers are getting ready to leave. I gather up Em and go to tell them goodbye. Momma puts her arm around my shoulders and gives me a quick hug. I head for the gate. I wait for the officers to leave and I secure the gate. Momma lets the dogs out. T runs to me, I hold Em really close and bend over to pet T. Em giggles at being almost upside down as T licks her face. The mosquitoes are coming out. Momma joins me in the porch swing with my brother. I let Em sit next to me, Momma puts my brother next to her. "We can't swing too high if they are sitting by themselves," Momma cautions.

"Momma. I know how to swing babies," I say indignantly.

She laughs. "I know you do. I also know how high you can swing."

"Momma, what about the money? What do we do with it? What do we need to do with it? I know part of it needs to go to church or charity or both, part of it should go to savings. What do we need? Momma, what if we get a car? It would be great to have a car, especially with two babies. I know we can't have a sports car. I know it has to be safe. But we could get a good used car. You tell me what you like and I'll research it and find us the best price. I'll look at gas mileage and

90

crash test results and resale statistics.

"We'll talk about this some more. I think our passengers are just about asleep on the porch swing. I want to make sure you have enough clothes and that you have art supplies. And yes, it looks like we will be getting you a bank account."

I stop the swing and gather up Em. My brother is also nodding off. Miss Bessie and Ms. Sanders are coming in, too, the dogs follow. I help Momma get the babies ready for bed. After they are changed and clean, I read them a short book and we put them to bed. Momma makes sure they are settled and I go into the living room where Miss Bessie and Ms. Sanders are. Miss Bessie is looking for a particular minister on television. Momma listens to the same program. Miss Bessie turns to me after she finds the channel.

"I have a surprise for you, dear. I understand that you and I have something else in common— we are both avid readers. Ms. Sanders sometimes laughs at me for reading the back of the cereal boxes, but I read everything. I do want to hear this minister tonight, but first, I want to show you the library. It is a joy and a refuge, to me."

I cannot believe my ears. Miss Bessie has enough books to call it a library and she is willing to let me read her books. Maybe she will let me borrow one. I find my words to answer.

"I would love to see the library, Miss Bessie. I was secretly hoping that you had one."

"If you find a book you like, I will trust you and let you borrow it. I do not loan my books as a regular practice."

I understand exactly what Miss Bessie means.

We are all going to the library, even Jasper and Teacup. We move quietly down the hall. This is like presents at Christmas. Miss Bessie stops at a darkened room and turns on the light. There are shelves and shelves of books, tall arched windows frame the room, one of them has a window seat, there is a special wooden ladder to reach the upper book shelves. There are leather couches and leather chairs. Oak tables with matching chairs and a large desk with a computer. Except for the computer, it is like stepping back in time. I take in the smell of leather and books. Miss Bessie begins telling me where each section is and how it is arranged. Every book is listed in her card catalog and she knows where it should be; they are numbered with the Dewey Decimal system. Some of the books are outdated, as to information, but they are still dear to Miss Bessie. She even has her first school books. When she went to school, students had to purchase their books. Some students struggled because their parents didn't have money at the beginning of the year. Then the schools tried to buy the books to give to the students like they do now. Miss Bessie attended a private school for girls after her first school would not let her study with the older students. I don't know where to start. Momma is going to stay in here with me. I know what section she is going to—cookbooks, especially cooking for large numbers of people. There is a whole section of art books. Some are so large that I may need Momma's help to get them to the table.

I start with Miss Bessie's old textbooks. I want to study the illustrations, particularly the figures and the grouping of figures. I like to draw people and animals, but I don't always get the proportions right. Sometimes, when I know that I've done it correctly, it still doesn't look right to me. It helps to see how other people have done it. Momma is thoroughly engrossed in her cookbooks. I write down the book that I was studying and the page number. I want to pick out a book to take with me. I find an old book that I haven't read. It is below my grade level but it also has great illustrations. I'll be able to read and study illustrations. Now I can just look at the books. I put my check out book on the desk. I start at one end of the library and begin to work my way around the room. Children's books, animals, history, math, science, law—of course, foreign languages, art, music, cooking and Momma, carpentry and non-fiction, fiction. I could just live here. I cannot imagine having a room full of books like this. Along with the computer, class projects would be no problem.

Momma will probably choose a cookbook. The time has passed too quickly. Miss Bessie comes in. "Have you found something you like, something to read later."

"I've found lots of books, Miss Bessie, but I only chose one. I chose it because I haven't read it and because I want to study the illustrations.

The reading will be the easy part. I think Momma will be choosing a cookbook."

Miss Bessie looks at the book that I have chosen. "It does have beautiful illustrations. I know someone who teaches at the art college in the park. In the summers, he teaches extra classes for younger students. Perhaps you could take lessons there."

Art lessons at the art college. I have no idea how much they cost. It would be good to be able to go. Illustrating would be a helpful skill for a veterinarian to have.

Momma is choosing a cookbook; it particularly has recipes for large groups. We write down which books we are taking and the date. We turn out the lights, after I get one more look around and run my hands over the nearest leather chair, and go to the living room to watch the news.

The announcer comes on, "Our top story tonight - police have solved several crimes with the arrest of two men late Thursday night. The men were apparently targeting single women, homeless people and families, the senior citizens and Hispanics in our community. Police got a break in solving the case and the subsequent arrest of the men when the last family fought back. They were also helped by two large white dogs, one of whom mysteriously disappeared right after the attack. Both the men and their wounds confirm that there were two dogs. Here is a photo taken by the police of the dogs in action."

The photo shows Jasper sitting on the one man and Juno biting the man at the door. The announcer ends the story with this comment. "Good work. The family is safe. The injured dog is recovering from a gunshot wound and two more criminals are off the street."

Miss Bessie has tears in her eyes. "That is Juno, that's her. I don't know how she came back but she did."

I look at Ms. Sanders. She nods in agreement. "Miss Bessie, I think Juno came back as an angel dog. I have one of her feathers, Ms. Sanders has found some, too. I want to check and see if there are some at the garden shed."

93

"That makes sense to me, an angel dog. I have found feathers in my room and feathers on the dog bed next to Jasper. I would love to go to the garden shed if you think you can, Miss Bessie replys.

"I guess we can go after the ceremony. I may sit in the car with the babies," Momma says.

Ms. Sanders is undecided. It may just be me and Miss Bessie.

It feels good to be in church with Miss Bessie and Ms. Sanders. The car was crowded but it sure felt like family. It looked like even Jasper and Teacup wanted to come, too. Maybe when my Daddy comes to visit, we could get Em and Lars baptized on the same Sunday. Miss Bessie and Ms. Sanders could stand with us.

We eat sandwiches, salad and leftover pizza for lunch. The babies really like the banana pudding. We barely have time to eat and get them cleaned up before we will have to leave for the ceremony. Jasper and Teacup have to have some outdoor time. They need to come with us. Jasper should get an award, too.

Just then, there is a horn honking out front. One of the officers is at the gate. I hand Em to Ms. Sanders, make sure the dogs are in and run out to open the gate. The officer stops just inside the gate. "We have an award for Jasper and the little black dog, as well as the other white dog. If you will ride with me, I have come to escort you, young lady, and the dogs, to the ceremony."

"I have to ask Momma." I take off for the house, even in my heels. Momma is on the porch.

"Momma, Momma, the officer wants to take me and the dogs to the ceremony. May I ride with him?"

"All right, Precious, you should be safe with him. Don't let Teacup get your dress dirty. I love you." I get a hug and kiss.

"I love you, too, Momma. Teacup will be good." I hurry and get the leashes. Jasper is excited, somehow he knows. Teacup wants to go to be with me. I wish I could have brushed them. I make sure Jasper's bandages are secure. We are ready to go, out the door. The officer has been patiently waiting. Miss Bessie walks out with me. I open the back door and put the dogs in. He motions for me to get up front.

"You take care of my girl and the dogs. I can't lose any of them," Miss Bessie says.

The officer replies, "Miss Bessie, you know my folks, you've known me all my life. I will take care of this young lady and the dogs. I will bring them safely back home or another officer will."

"Well, we're going to be making a side trip to that old playhouse/garden shed after the ceremony. Just this wonderful young lady and me and the dogs."

"Miss Bessie, I don't want you going over there by yourselves. I'll go with you. I'll be off then. I'll be your escort."

"That will be fine. I won't keep you. We'll see you there."

I hug Miss Bessie and get in. Jasper is laying down and Teacup is up against him.

"Are you buckled in? Let's go." He backs out of the driveway and we head to the station. This is my second time in a police car this week. At least for now, Jasper and Teacup get to pretend to be part of the K-9 unit. "I don't think we've had a cocker spaniel in the K-9 unit before," he remarks.

"Teacup wanted to bite them. She let us know they were coming. She stayed with the babies. She's only been with us this week. Do you know a good veterinarian in this area? I know Teacup is too young for most shots or to be spayed, but no one has looked at her yet. I doubt the woman who gave her to us had money for her shots. She could be a backyard breeder puppy mill puppy."

"Well, I'll tell you what we can do. You know all of the dogs in the K-9 unit go to the vet on a regular basis. The police department will pay for Teacup's first checkup with our vet. I'll work out the details with Miss Bessie and your Mother. I'll let them know her schedule. I think you'll like this vet. It may be the one that Miss Bessie already uses for Jasper."

"Thank you, sir. That would be wonderful. I want to make sure Teacup gets started on her vaccinations, especially the ones for parvo and distemper. She doesn't appear to have flea problems but a Dawn soap solution or bath will kill these. Because of her size, I'd probably give her a cat size dose of flea medicine."

"My goodness! You certainly know a lot about pets."

"Thank you. I go to the library and read on a regular basis. I want to be a veterinarian when I get out of college. I know I'll have to go to college at least eight years, and longer if I specialize. I think I'll probably open a practice in a more rural area and treat large animals, cows and horses, as well as cats and dogs. I know there's beginning to be a shortage of large animal veterinarians in the US. Treating farm animals, you'd also learn about birds because of the chickens."

"I wish my nephew would read more often." I know who this officer is. I bet his nephew is the boy I beat in the race.

"Sir, does your nephew like to run?"

"Yes, he does. Are you the one who raced against him this week?"

I describe Ben to him.

"Yes, that's him. I'm sure of it. Are you so set on being a veterinarian that I couldn't talk you into a career in law enforcement?"

We both laugh. "No, sir, I've wanted to be a veterinarian for a long time now. If it was up to me, we'd have a house full of pets, all kinds, just from the animals that other people put out. That will be the hard part about being a veterinarian. I know there will be a limit. A limit on the number of pets that I can have and a limit to the number that I can help. Right now, I'm just real thankful to have Teacup and for Jasper."

We pull into a space at the station. We get out and I open the back door to get Jasper and Teacup. The officer shows me a grassy area where I can walk them before we go into the building. We will go in with the officer through the officer's entrance.

The other officers smile and joke as we come in. "Recruits are getting younger and younger. Now that looks like old Jasper."

"It is Jasper. This is the young woman who helped us capture those two scoundrels with the broken hands. But she is determined to be a veterinarian. I tried to talk her into joining the police force. She goes to the library and reads all the time, too. She's the one who beat my nephew in the race at school."

"She beat your nephew? Well, she has to be really fast. Are we taking cocker spaniels now? We could send them into really small spaces."

I find my voice. "Teacup will not be joining the force, either. I am hoping she will live a long life and I will have her when I start college. I know she probably will not live until I finish college and veterinary school, but I have her for now."

The officers look at me. "Thank you for your help. Do not feel bad about injuring those two men. They were trying to hurt you and your Mother. You had to stop them."

Teacup has made herself right at home and is sitting in one of the officer's laps. Jasper is getting petting. "The K-9 dogs are going to know we petted other dogs and had them in the office."

The captain comes in. "Good afternoon, I didn't realize that you were here. We're ready to start." We move into the conference room. Momma and the babies, Miss Bessie and Ms. Sanders, are all waiting. There is a photographer. The other officers come in and sit down. The captain begins talking. "We are here today to honor a young woman," he says my whole name, "and two dogs, Jasper and Teacup, for apprehending two criminals. Because of their bravery, we have been able to solve several cases. It is also because of this young woman's quick thinking, that the department knew that Miss Bessie had been attacked. Because of this, we have several awards to present." He continues.

"Old Jasper - this medal for pursuing a criminal even though you were injured." Jasper steps forward, sits, and looks at the captain. The captain places the medal around his neck. Everyone claps and Jasper wags his tail. Miss Bessie beams.

"Teacup- for letting the family know that trouble was coming." I step forward with Teacup in my arms and hold her up for her medal. She tries to kiss the Captain. The photographer snaps the picture. Everyone laughs and claps.

"Stay up here," the Captain says.

"Not only did this young lady manage to apprehend two criminals by catching their hands in the old rusty rat traps, she had the presence of mind to record the attack and to listen to what the criminals were saying. By recording the attack, she will help convict them. By notifying the 911 operator about the earlier attack on Miss Bessie and finding the address, she saved Miss Bessie. If we could find Juno, she would get a medal as well. On behalf of the Police Department, the community and the Crime stopper's program, we present you with this medal for Heroism and this check for $15,000." The Captain puts the medal around my neck and hands me the check. Everyone claps and takes pictures. I hug Teacup and manage to tell the Captain, "Thank you."

"Would you like to say a few words?" he asks.

I take the microphone and hold Teacup with one hand.

"Thank you all, again. A lot has happened this week. Just know that Momma and I will put this check to good use. We will not squander or waste it. The money is certainly an unexpected blessing."

Everyone claps again. The photographer has me to pose with the dogs, the Captain and the officers who first arrived on the scene. Then with the Captain and the dogs and finally, just with the dogs. Miss Bessie wants a picture of Momma and me, the babies and the dogs. The officer takes a picture of Momma, me, Ms. Sanders, Miss Bessie, the babies and the dogs. Now we get to have refreshments.

There is cake and punch, cookies and dog biscuits- Jasper size and Teacup size. I give Jasper one large biscuit and two little ones for Teacup. I put their biscuits on a plate so they will not get crumbs everywhere. Em and my brother like the punch. Em tries to grab a dog biscuit. They each get a bit of cake. Momma comes and gives me a hug. Many of the officers come to thank me, to talk and to shake my hand. This kind of attention is almost overwhelming to me.

Miss Bessie comes to me and asks if I am ready to go. I am more than ready. The officer is going to take us to the garden shed and then home. Jasper and Teacup are coming, too.

I hug Momma and Ms. Sanders and the babies goodbye, tell them that I love them. I get Teacup and Jasper, make sure they haven't left dog biscuit crumbs everywhere. The officer asks if we are ready. Miss Bessie and I walk back through the hallway to the officers' and out to the squad car. The officers pet Teacup and Jasper. "You are all welcome to come back and visit anytime," they say.

Suddenly I have a thought. "When I graduate and get my veterinary license, I could be the veterinarian for the K-9 unit. I could help in that way."

The Captain smiles. "We will be happy to have you with us as a veterinarian. Maybe the vet would let you do an internship. When you are ready, come back and see me. I'll put in a good word for you."

"Thank you, sir. I will remember."

I make sure Miss Bessie is settled and buckled in the front seat. The officer puts Jasper and Teacup in the back seat. I get in back with them. Jasper lays down and puts his head in my lap, next to Teacup. It will not take long to get there. The closer we get, the more my stomach ties in knots.

The officer pulls into the driveway and around to the door. Jasper and Teacup are excited. The officer opens the back car door and we get out. He goes to the front and helps Miss Bessie out. I walk the dogs around the yard. Something white is shining in the grass beneath the boards of the steps. I walk the dogs over there and reach between the boards. One of the feathers is large. Miss Bessie is watching. She smiles. "Do you have a pocket?" I hand it to her. She holds it up for the officer. "Angel dog feathers, from Juno, my precious dog Juno."

"Everyone said that there were two dogs. We do have that photo. I'll find another feather. It would definitely be interesting to see what the crime lab could make of it."

I get out my keys. It is hard to turn the lock because the door is so damaged. Teacup is wagging her tail. The officer offers his help.

"Do you want me to hold the dogs or to try to open the door?"

I hand him the keys. After a few minutes, the lock turns and the door opens. The officer holds the door open and offers Miss Bessie his arm. She steps in slowly. From the expression on her face and how she is looking around, I can tell Miss Bessie is going back in time. She is remembering playing here. I wait for her to say something. Jasper is sniffing everything. Teacup stays close beside me. She remembers, too. Finally, Miss Bessie speaks. "I am so glad you had bars on the windows and the security door. I like the screens and the curtains. Ms. Sanders' son does windows and carpentry work. I will get him to replace the glass in the windows and repair the door. We may to replace the door. I will call him tomorrow." She continues. "Thank God you had the presence of mind to use these old rat traps. Well, let's see what else is here. Have you ever explored this room in the daylight, dear?"

I shake my head. "We only came at night time. We were real excited the night that we found the electric socket."

"There is something else here, too. Did you ever notice this door over here?" Miss Bessie is right. There is a door.

"My father insisted that we have this room when the playhouse was built. He didn't want us coming in the house dirty and tracking in dirt."

Miss Bessie takes out her key ring. There is an old fashioned hollow key on it. The door knob is silver colored, but dark, and has flowers and vines embossed on it. The same design is on the edges of the door plate. How could we have not seen this door? How could it have survived all of this time and not been damaged?

Miss Bessie turns the key. It is a little rusty but it catches and I hear the lock turning. The door cracks open.

"Oh, my goodness, Miss Bessie! It's beautiful!"

Inside, is the most beautiful little girl bathroom that I have ever seen. There is a white pedestal sink, an old fashioned looking toilet and a shower area. The walls have beadboard wainscoting halfway up except for the shower area. The floor tiles are pale green with flecks of brown and blue and yellow. It looks like moss or the different shades of grass. The wall tiles around the shower are pale, pearlized, pink. They seem to glow in the sunlight. There is one small, round window near the ceiling with several panes in it. Everything is dusty. Miss Bessie goes to the sink and turns the knob, a brass and porcelain knob. The faucet is arched and brass. There is a chugging, coughing noise from air in the pipes. Water has not run through them in a long, long time. Suddenly, brown water explodes from the faucet and gurgles noisily into the sink; then the water runs clear. Miss Bessie smiles, "After all these years and it still works."

I shake my head in disbelief. All these nights we spent here in misery, either not having water or wishing for a bathroom and it was here all the time. Momma will have to see this.

Miss Bessie walks around the garden shed looking at different things while I still marvel at the bathroom. She shows me where the electrical outlets are in the rest of the shed. Then she says, "We will come back another day, clean up and get this place in order. This will be an extra, private space for you. I will get everything fixed."

"Oh, thank you, Miss Bessie. This would be like having my own little house. I have always felt safe here; I have always liked it, until the other night."

"You will be safe again, child. You will be safe again. I assure you. You've had a long day. It's time to go for now."

Through all of this, the officer has been silent. At times, he was outside, looking for feathers. "Miss Bessie," he asks, "don't you still own all of this?"

She nods yes.

"Miss Bessie, I think in the tax records, it is listed as part of the church property. We looked it up."

"I'll have to check on that. At one time, we had given it to the church for expansion, but it was to come back to our family if the church didn't use it."

I find the letter and the envelope from the church and show it to her. She laughs. "The address is correct though. I have been paying the property taxes, so that will not be an issue. Let's go outside and walk a bit."

We go outside. The officer locks the door and returns my keys. "We're going to walk the property line and look for the fence or remnants of the fence. Come on Jasper, Little Teacup. Help an old lady get her boundaries." Miss Bessie begins walking to the edge of the property. The dogs follow eagerly, happy about the adventure.

I did not realize how far the property goes. I follow at times, walk ahead at other times. I can let my mind drift and imagine myself back in time, running the property with Miss Bessie, only she wouldn't be Miss Bessie. I can go further back and imagine Indians here, children running with their dogs, gathering berries, practicing throwing spears and shooting bows and arrows. I would be the girl who took care of the dogs and the horses, who helped dig the clay for the pottery and wove special baskets. I would look after the orphan children. We would be a special family within our tribe.

Miss Bessie is beside me. "Am I losing you to another time, child?"

I have to laugh. "Almost, I was just thinking about all the people who lived here before us, especially the children. I was also thinking about you running through these fields and that I think," I pause a bit, "I think we would have been good friends. We probably would have gotten in trouble for being independent and wanting to learn so much, but the world did change."

"That is probably one of the nicest things anyone has said to me in a long time. I can't run these fields with you, but we can become good friends. Age does not keep someone from nurturing friendship." Miss Bessie gives me a hug. We are almost back where we started.

I can tell that Miss Bessie is tired. I think the dogs want a nap, too.

We head back into the police car. Soon we are at the gate. Ms. Sanders left it open for us. I get out with the dogs. We will wait while the officer gets Miss Bessie to the door.

I tell him goodbye as he stops, and thank you for everything. I wasn't really sure I could go back there.

"You have to come back and visit, young lady. You know where we are. My nephew comes down to the station sometimes. You would be welcome to come and watch us train dogs. You just give us a call."

"That would be wonderful, sir. I hear there's also a stable downtown for the horses."

"There is at that, although I've never had any desire to join the mounted patrol."

"Take care, sir. Thank you for everything." He gives me his contact numbers. He backs out, waves goodbye and is gone. I shut the gate and let the dogs run free. They roam the yard a bit and head to the porch. Momma lets them in.

"The babies are sleeping. You go take a nap, too. Then we'll decide about tonight. I hear there is a beautiful bathroom we didn't know about. I'll wait for you to tell me about it. I love you."

"I love you, too, Momma. I am tired." Teacup wastes no time heading for the bedroom. Once again, I am thankful for this bed and this bedroom, for this place of refuge. Grateful for this house, for Miss Bessie and for Ms. Sanders, good did come out of evil. I am asleep almost before my head hits the pillow. T gives a long puppy sigh and stretches out along side of me. Jasper snores a little and then turns over. Fortunately, he has his own bed in the parlor and one in Miss Bessie's room. Quiet. We all sleep.

I awaken, rested. Momma is changing babies. T is beside me, sound asleep on her back, all of her paws in the air. T falls to one side and wakes herself up, tail wagging. I rub her belly. She jumps off the bed and runs to find Jasper. I hear her whining to get into his bed. I quickly get dressed. Momma hands Em over to me. Em wraps her arms around my neck and snuggles close. It is almost dinner time. We go into the kitchen and Ms. Sanders shoos us out. "I am doing dinner tonight with Miss Bessie. You go into the parlor with your Momma."

Em and I go sit on the couch. Momma comes in with Lars and sits beside me. "You've had a long day, child. Your Father would have been so proud of you at the ceremony. Now that we'll have an address, we should hear from him soon. But we can talk and dream about that later. That time will come. Tell me about this bathroom we never found and we could have used, so many times."

"Momma, it's just beautiful. It is the most beautiful bathroom that I have ever seen. You'll have to see it." I describe it for her as best I can. I tell her about the little window and the sunlight illuminating the room, the pearly glow of the tiles, the absolute miracle of the water still working. The other miracle, that no one broke into the shed and trashed the bathroom for the copper and brass. Then I tell her the best part—that Miss Bessie is going to fix all of the damage and help me fix it up, that is going to be my space. I also mention that she showed me where all of the electrical sockets are.

"Well, I will have to see this bathroom. How did you feel about being there after all that had happened?"

"I wasn't sure at first that I could go back there. But I knew that Miss Bessie really wanted to go. My stomach was all in knots the closer we got to the shed. I knew the officer and Miss Bessie and the dogs would not let anything happen to me. Besides, it was daylight. I wanted to see the shed in the daylight; I wanted to see the shed the way Miss Bessie saw it and I did. I could see it as a playhouse. I could see her playing there with her sister and her baby brother. I could see her running the boundaries of their property. I could see her standing in the shower, washing her feet so she could put her stockings on and go back to her house. I could feel the joy that she had felt being there. You will have to see the playhouse in the daylight, Momma, and the bathroom."

Miss Bessie has come in. "Yes, you will have to see it all in the daylight. And I did do all of the things you mentioned. That and a whole lot more. It will be good to have children running the property again and washing up in the shower. If I think I've still got the furniture from the playhouse in storage. We'll have to get it out and clean it up just like we did the bicycles and the pedal car. But for now, it's time for dinner."

Dinner smells have been filling the house all afternoon since we got back. Dinner - Momma and I still don't have groceries and cleaning supplies for the new house.

We are having ham and turnip greens, sweet potatoes with raisins, fruit salad and baked squash. There is also a tray of deviled eggs. This is like Christmas or Easter. Momma and I put the babies in their high chairs while I fill their plates. We all sit down. Ms. Sanders puts candlesticks on the table and lights them. Miss Bessie says the blessing. She says how thankful she is for us and that we have come into her life. We are thankful for her, too. We are also thankful for angel dogs and rusty rat traps. She gives thanks for the food. Now we can eat.

Em and Lars are fascinated by the candlelight. It is pretty, but I would not want to have to light the house with it. The babies are dropping food on the floor and I can't see it. Finally, Miss Bessie says, "OK, I can't see my food. We have to have light for my old eyes."

Ms. Sanders laughs, "Where is your romanticism, Miss Bessie?" She turns the lights back on. I blow the candles out.

Miss Bessie responds, "I think it went the way of my eyesight. I'll read about it in books and leave it to these younger people we have with us."

"You can still have romanticism, Miss Bessie," I say, "your house is romantic."

"Oh, I guess it is at that. Alright, I'll go with living in a romantic house."

Lars and Em are banging their trays. I offer them more green beans and mashed sweet potatoes. I give Em a small bowl of applesauce with a spoon. I give my brother regular fruit salad in his bowl.

It seems like its been forever since I had baked ham. Momma does have groceries and cleaning supplies at the new house. She went to the store while I was sleeping. She is enjoying the ham, too.

Conversation turns to the ceremony from this afternoon. Miss Bessie knew several of the officers and their families. Momma thought Em and my brother behaved really well. Miss Bessie agreed. Momma said people complimented her on her children. I said I thought the dogs were really well behaved. Miss Bessie accepted an award for Juno, as well. She is going to put both of the awards in the china cabinet, in the dining room. She said our pictures may be in the newspaper or there may be a television news story about us but the information will be very limited. I know she doesn't want us to worry. She says they will not give out our address or say that we are homeless. We are not homeless now.

There are three kinds of dessert to choose from - that would suggest that we are wealthy. Hard choice. I choose banana pudding for Em and Lars; they can easily eat this by themselves. The chocolate cake and the peanut butter cake will be going with us to our new home or at least a part of them will. I am going to eat banana pudding, too.

"Ms. Sanders, we have probably gained a few pounds from eating all of these desserts, but I sure have enjoyed them." Ms. Sanders nods in agreement. Miss Bessie continues, "We're both going to have to have running shoes. And Jasper can't walk with us, yet. Maybe we can just take the pedal car out around the block a couple of times with Jasper along for the ride. That should burn some calories."

Momma says, "Maybe I can come and walk with you sometimes. I know my girl is going to be running." She looks at me and smiles.

I reply, "I will be running. Just as soon as I find my way around the neighborhood of our new house. I haven't decided if I'm going to run by the cousin's house. I am going to give you a map of the route or routes I run, the days I run each route and the time that I expect to be running. I didn't do that before, but I will now. We need to know where the other one is, even after we get Daddy back."

Momma agrees. She looked at me when I mentioned Daddy. I can begin to think about him again. He will come back. Em and Lars want more pudding. Momma says they can have it. I want coffee. Momma says I can have it. I get coffee for Miss Bessie and Ms. Sanders, first.

I used to get my Daddy's coffee, too. Momma hasn't decided if she wants coffee. I sit down and Em makes a grab for my coffee. Fortunately, her reach is not enough. "Em, precious one, we are not going to put coffee in your sippy cup. We are not that liberal." She laughs as though she understands and claps her hands over her mouth.

Miss Bessie says, "You folks are going to have to pick a day to come back and have dinner with us once a week. We want to meet that Daddy when he comes back, too, and give him a ride in the pedal car."

"I think Daddy will fit in the pedal car. I don't think that he's too tall."

Momma looks at me "We need to get these babies cleaned up, gather up our stuff and..." She pauses, "go home." You have a new room to see. We have to meet with our worker on Monday so that she can see the house. We go to court on Tuesday about Em."

My mind is racing - go to court about Em, are they trying to take Em? Momma sees my face.

"The court hearing is to confirm that we want Em, that we are taking care of her and that her Mother gave her to us voluntarily. Her Mother may or may not come to court, but Em has to come to court. Our worker will be coming as well as an attorney. The attorney is ours. Em will have her own attorney."

"You are going to have two busy days. I know you're nervous about court. Folks always get nervous about court. If you like, I could come, too. I can still practice and take cases."

I don't even ask Momma; I just blurt it out. "Miss Bessie, I would love it if you would come with us. Just thinking about court ties my stomach in knots. And I don't want to give up Em, even to her Mother." Momma looks at me again. "I'm serious, Momma. Em needs us. Her Mother gave her to us and I don't want her trying to take her back."

"Sweetie, I'm glad that you feel so strongly about Em; she needs for us to be in her corner. But we still have to go to court and we still have to listen to the judge."

"I'll go Momma, and I'll listen and I'll be respectful to the judge, but Em belongs with us." I pick up Em and head to the bedroom.

I hear Miss Bessie still talking. "I don't see why the judge wouldn't leave Emily with you. I think a lot will depend on whether her mother shows up, and what happens with that. She also has to have a father somewhere. Do you know which judge you will see?"

"I have no clue as to which judge we will see. I hope when we get there that it is someone you know." I hear Momma pick up Lars and head my way. Em is clean and in her pajamas. She reaches out for Lars as he passes by. I set her in the youth bed with toys and start gathering all of the baby things. It is Sunday evening and we have only been here since late Thursday, yet it looks like the babies live here. I have my small suitcase and Teacup's few toys, her food and her bowls. I have to remember and take the book that I checked out from Miss Bessie. Em and my brother are babbling to each other as though Momma and I are not even here. Teacup is sitting on the floor watching and listening to them, keeping her eye on me to make sure that I do not leave her. Finally, I have everything. I sit down on the bed and scoop up T, then flop back on the bed. T gets as close as she can and puts her head on my shoulder.

"We're not leaving you, T, you're coming. You'll be able to run around the front and the backyard, everything is fenced." T sighs one of her puppy sighs and closes her eyes.

"Let me make sure that I have everything and then I think we are ready to start loading the car. You and T cannot go to sleep yet."

"Come on T, that's our cue to move." I start to get up. T moves to the edge of the bed and jumps down. I hear Jasper wagging his tail. I begin moving all of our things to the door.

"Don't go just yet," Miss Bessie calls from the parlor. "I have to make sure we have your new address. Jasper is sure going to miss that little Teacup."

"We're not gone, Miss Bessie. Babies have lots of stuff. I'm just getting everything to the door," I assure her. Momma is in the kitchen with Ms. Sanders, dividing up the cakes. Ms. Sanders is sending us out with pizza, chicken salad sandwiches and banana pudding. It is neatly wrapped and packed in a box. I get the keys from Ms. Sanders and load everything. Then I join Miss Bessie and Jasper in the parlor.

"I can't begin to tell you, child, how much I've enjoyed having you and your family and how much I appreciate you." She gives me a hug.

"Miss Bessie, I feel so comfortable here. It feels like home, like a Grandmother's house. I feel that I have known you for a long time and yet I know I haven't. I am scared about court."

"Court is its own place, with its own set of rules. We have to abide by them. I will be there with you."

Momma and Ms. Sanders come in. "I think we are ready to load babies, one tall daughter, and a black, curly puppy," Momma says. T wags her tail. I hug Miss Bessie again. I pat Jasper, and kiss his big head, holding his face in my hands. I hug Ms. Sanders. I pick up Em and grab T's leash. We are going to our new house. Momma has my brother. Miss Bessie kisses each of the babies goodbye.

"Oh, Little Ones, it was so good to have babies in the house again. The two of you will have to come back by yourselves and spend the night. We'll have a sleepover for babies. On Tuesday, you let T spend the day here with Jasper so they can have time together while we go to court."

"Miss Bessie, Momma says, "that seems like a lot for you to do. You're already giving us a ride to court and being with us in court. You've taken us in these last few days. Are you sure that you want to do doggie daycare?"

Doggie daycare. That's a good name for it. Yes, we want to do doggie daycare. We have all gotten attached to Little Miss Teacup. On Tuesday, when we pick you up for court, you will bring Teacup. Ms. Sanders will drop us off at court and bring Teacup back over here. Court may take awhile. We will call when we are done." Momma agrees to the plan. We head to the car and buckle Em and Lars in. I get between them and hold Teacup. They will be asleep by the time we get home. Home. We have a home again. Bedrooms, a bathroom whenever I want and a kitchen. No more packing up after dinner. The food in the refrigerator will be ours. I can get up in the middle of the night and raid the refrigerator. I can have cold water. No one will take my after school snacks. No cigarette or beer smell in the house. Teacup and I can sit on the back steps and look at the stars. We will be safe. Maybe one night Jasper can come spend the night and have a playdate with T. We are almost there.

We pull into the driveway. I unbuckle Em and my brother. He is reaching for me and Em is asleep. I put him on one hip and grab T's leash. Ms. Sanders stays with Em. Momma begins to empty the trunk. She opens the door. It is beautiful. I had forgotten how special our furniture is to me. I want to sit down and take it all in, but I need to help bring in the last of our things. I put my brother in the crib with the Spiderman sheets. Em's crib has pink kittens on the sheets. Lars lays down but keeps his eyes open. Momma brings in the baby bags. Only our bags and books are left. "Baby or bags?" Momma asks. "Baby," I reply. Momma will get the bags while I get Em.

Em is still asleep. I tell Ms. Sanders thank you and shut the door. "Goodnight, Child. We'll see you Tuesday for sure." Momma shuts the trunk. We watch her back out. Momma latches the gate. We walk to the door, Momma's arm around me. Momma puts the bags on the table and holds out her hands to take Em. I hand her over. I go sit on the couch. Our couch, in our living room. The couch has a slight storage, closed up room smell, but that does not matter. Momma comes back. "We can clean it tomorrow as we unpack everything else. The important thing is, we have a home."

Momma and I sit on the couch, her arms around me. There is no need for words. Finally she speaks. "Your bed is set up and your chest of drawers is in there as well as your dresser and the little armoire. We will get another larger armoire as you need it. Perhaps later on, we will have a house with closets. Your other, more personal things, have been left for you to place. I figured T would sleep on your bed. I would prefer not to move furniture tonight because the babies are asleep. Go look at your room and come back when you are ready. I'm going to put away the chicken salad and the banana pudding, then we can watch television. Now git!"

"I love you, Momma."

"I love you, too, Precious, I love you, too."

I don't know where she found them, but Momma found curtains for all 7 windows in my room. They are cream colored with large red and pink flowers with dark green leaves. They have an old fashioned look... about them. Miss Bessie must have donated my curtains! I have part of Miss Bessie with me. My bed, Momma's old bed from when she was little. It sits high and has metal wheels on the bottom. I doubt Teacup will ever be able to jump up here. I can make her some doggie steps. I know Miss Bessie would probably know how to make them. All my boxes are stacked on the floor at the foot of the bed. Everything is fine for now. I like having the laundry room on the other side of my room with the back door. I take T off the bed and we head back to the living room.

Momma offers me hot tea. We never drink coffee after 8 PM. She also offers me the option of eating pizza - sitting on the couch eating pizza watching television in our living room on a Sunday night. It has been so long since we were able to do this. The program is the one where the lady helps people to go through their stuff and clean their house. Then they have a yard sale. She takes the money and redoes a room or two in their house. It always looks better when she is done and I have never seen the people be unhappy with what she has done. We don't need anyone to help us clean and I think now, we will eventually be able to buy another house, even with taking in Em.

I don't usually watch the news, but Momma says we may be on the news tonight. It is the same announcer from the night before. "There was a ceremony today to recognize the young lady who helped capture the two criminals. The dogs were also honored. Crimestoppers presented her with a check and a medal. Miss Bessie received medals for her two dogs and the cocker spaniel also received a medal. Here we see the cocker spaniel, Teacup, receiving her medal and trying to kiss the captain.

111

Then everyone, including the dogs, had refreshments." It shows Jasper and Teacup eating dog biscuits. The announcer finishes with some comments by the police captain. They did not give out names or our new address. We are still safe. Momma and I watch the rest of the news. Then we take Teacup out front one last time before we go to bed. Truns the yard, exploring all the corners. It will be nice to have porch chairs. Maybe a double rocker like the ones from the man at the amusement park. We could put a porch swing at one end, the far end away from the driveway. I can already imagine swinging in it. Tomorrow, I'll have to check the sun and see where it will be best to plant the tomato plants. I give T my last bite of pizza crust. We all go in and Momma locks the door. She gives me a hug. "I have something for you. Hold out your hand." I close my eyes and hold out my hand, giggling. Teacup is sitting on my feet and it tickles. Momma places something small and hard and cold in my hand. "Welcome, home, Precious, I love you." I know before I open my eyes what it is. Momma has given me a house key. My very own house key. Momma is saying that I am grown up and responsible enough to have my own house key.

"Thank you, Momma. I love you, too. I will not lose it." I get Teacup and my goodnight kiss and hug from Momma, then head for bed. It is quiet in our house. I tiptoe past the sleeping babies. I still have to brush my teeth. I get my toothbrush, T comes, too. Momma has already set everything up, even the shampoo and conditioner. There are new fluffy towels—pink, green, blue, pale yellow. I've already had one shower today but it is tempting to take another one just to use the towels. Teacup is going to sleep on the floor, small black and white tiles sat at an angle in a herringbone pattern. The walls are pink tile two thirds of the way up, then outlined in black tile with white tile to the ceiling. I get T some water for tonight, not too much, maybe she will sleep through the night and not have to go out. Back down the quiet hallway to my new sanctuary. I turn on my lamp and turn off the overhead. I put T on the bed and get undressed. I'll decide tomorrow how to arrange my drawers. I can lay in bed and still see the moon and the stars. Lights out. T is already asleep. I rub her silky fur one last time. Sleep. In my own bed, clean sheets, ceiling fan, sleeping pup. Where is the cat?

The sun is pouring in. T is still asleep, on her back, feet in the air. We have slept late. Suddenly, there is banging on my door, low, close to the floor. T is wagging her tail. I throw on my nightshirt and open the door. My brother is standing there, all on his own. He grins. "Doggie, doggie, doggie." I pick him up and give him a kiss. "Down." I put him down. He runs back down the hall, his hand trailing the wall. My brother is walking and running on his own. Amazing.

I put on my sandals and shorts. T and I head for the back door. I can smell fresh coffee in the kitchen. I let T out and she runs to the very back of the yard. I go ahead and get coffee, then follow T into the yard. There are plum trees at the back, one on either side of the shed. There is a crepe myrtle with gracefully curved branches and a tree I don't know. The tree that I don't know has soft green needles and pink flowers about the size of the head of a finishing nail. We could put a bird feeder back here. There is an old swing set. It needs the rust removed and a paint job, but it has enough room for two baby swings and a swing bar for me. There is a place along the fence, heading toward the driveway, where we might be able to put the tomato plants. I have to think about it a minute to make sure of my directions. The east side of the house is shaded in back. There is only a narrow space between our house and the fence. I could put the tomatoes at the back of the yard on the south side, if there is not too much shade from the plum trees, but I don't want them behind the shed. I want to be able to see them from the back door. We are going to have to have a lawn mower. I sit on the back stoop, drinking coffee and petting T. I have so missed having a regular life. We both stretch and get up. Breakfast is calling through the screen door. Bacon and eggs and biscuits and messy babies.

My brother is trying to get into his highchair by himself. I move the tray and he scrambles up. Em looks at me and tries to pet T. I secure her in her chair. They get to have eggs first, then torn bacon bits. Biscuits will be last. I butter the biscuits and add a little honey. It is much easier to feed children when they want to do most of it themselves. Messy, but easier, plus it gives me a chance to eat.

Momma says Ms. Jackson is coming at 10. She will ~~tattoo~~ talk with us and look at the house, now that we have moved in. I finish my breakfast and coffee and sweep up the food bits that the babies dropped. I put them in Ts dish and wipe the floor. "You want to clean up babies or wash dishes?" Momma asks. "I'll take babies, one at a time." I pick up my brother and carry him to his room. He laughs as I wash his hands and face. I see the tape player in a box. I manage to hold him and get it plugged in. I find my favorite tape. I sit him on the floor with toys. He waves his hands as the tape comes on. He remembers. Em is fussing a little when I get back, even though Momma is talking to her.

"Em, you are not alone. You are being taken care of. You cannot fuss," I say. She looks at me and bangs her tray. "Now!" she says emphatically, "Now!" Momma and I have to laugh. Em is definitely going to want to run things. I swing her in the air as I lift her up and she squeals happily.

Teacup cries when we get to the room because of the baby gate. Lars is glad to see us. I step over the gate. T will just have to wait.

Soon I am ready to set Em down to play. Momma comes in. "I am going to straighten up and arrange their toys. I have missed hearing that tape," Momma says. "I have, too, Momma. I'll see how much of my room I can put in order before 10. What will Ms. Jackson be looking for anyway?"

"She just wants to be sure that we have enough space, we all have beds, we have the necessary appliances, there are groceries and dishes and baby toys. We have utilities. All of our things and the baby things."

"OK, then I can relax and save all of my worrying for court tomorrow. I don't want to think about that at all, Momma. I will decide what I'm going to wear and I will pick out outfits for the babies."

"You always look nice when you are dressed up, Sweetheart. I know the babies will look nice, too."

I pet Teacup as I climb over the gate. She has been a patient puppy. She is looking at me intently. She runs down the hallway to the pantry door and jumps against the door. I open the pantry door and the screen door. Teacup dashes out to the back of the yard. Soon she is banging the screen door. Teacup is such a smart puppy, knowing she needed to go out. I let her back in so that we can get busy.

I am almost overwhelmed by the boxes and plastic crates. I don't remember what is in all these containers. I plop onto the bed with Teacup and one of the boxes. She sniffs eagerly as I open it - knee socks, winter clothes - bottom drawer for now. The pants may be too short for next year. Where are my spring and summer things? I do a quick check of the boxes until I find them. The shorts are at the bottom of the box. I can look at some of them and tell that they are too short. Some of my tee shirts are like old friends - I'm glad to see them. Momma can give some of my shorts to someone else. I let Teacup play in the empty box, chasing her tail. There are two boxes left - books and journals and sketch books, paints, charcoal, rulers, craypas, colored pencils, crayons, different papers and my little wooden figure. That box can go on my table. My little brass lamp is there, along with my heart shaped clock radio. I put the crystal pink angel night light in the bathroom. I like to turn out all of the lights when I sleep. I don't know about the babies. I know my brother is used to the dark. Teacup barks. Our worker, Ms. Jackson, must be here. I will let Momma answer the door. I wait, listening, savoring the moment. Momma is answering the door at our house. Teacup is barking and wagging her tail. I hear Momma greeting Ms. Jackson. I pick up Teacup and walk to the dining room. My brother is standing at the gate, banging. "Out, out." He says excitedly. Em is waiting to see if he gets out or not.

"Good morning, dear, it is good to see you. I was explaining to your Mother that I just need to see all of the rooms. I hear these babies. Teacup looks happy." She reaches out and pets her, "Could I hold her a minute?"

"Of course, but her paws may be dirty, she's been outside."

"I'll be fine. Come here little black dog."

Teacup is wagging all over. She licks Ms. Jackson in the face. Ms. Jackson pets her and hands her back, saying, "I also need to take pictures. Maybe you can help me with that."

Momma compliments me. "She takes really good photographs. She's been our family photographer for years."

"Where do you want to start, Ms. Jackson?"

"Let's just start here in the living room." Ms. Jackson and I move through the house, room by room, taking pictures. Teacup follows. We get an extra picture of Em and Lars smiling and standing at the baby gate. We go back to the living room. T and I plop down on the couch. Ms. Jackson sits down gracefully and begins talking. "Tomorrow is a big day, not only for you, but also for Em. I will be advocating for Em to stay with you. They will be formally asking if you will accept custody of Em. If things go well, you may be asked later if you will adopt her. Her Mother may come; she may not. She may choose to be represented only by her lawyer as she voluntarily placed Em with you and we have her letter. I can and will testify that all of the needs of the children have been met, and that your daughter attended school regularly. She not only passed but had excellent grades. I will also mention the award she received for running and the one for heroism." She looks at me. "Answer any question the Judge asks, yes, ma'am, no ma'am, yes, sir, no, sir or yes your honor, no your honor. I know you will dress appropriately. The babes may or may not have to remain in the court room the entire time. The Judge may ask to speak with you alone in his/her office or chambers. Do not be alarmed if this happens, nothing is wrong. Do you have any questions?"

"No, Ms. Jackson, not really. I'm trying not to be nervous. In some ways, I just want to throw up already."

"Sweetheart," Momma says, "I will be there and so will Miss Bessie. It is going to be all right." She gives me a hug.

"Momma, if it is OK, T and I are going to go back to my room so I can get it arranged. That will help me to deal with tomorrow. Order out of chaos."

"Smart child," Ms. Jackson says. "I will see you tomorrow."

"Thank you, Ms. Jackson." I am grateful to be able to retreat to my room. Em and Lars are still playing. I step over the gate and restart the music, giving each of them a kiss.

I love the windows in my room. I can have the outdoors and still be inside. I put the summer clothes that still fit in the first drawer. I put socks and intimates in the top two drawers that are not as deep. Somewhere, I have skirts and dresses and dress shoes. The armoire!

116

I had forgotten about it. I open it up. Momma must have hung them up. They are all here, still in plastic. I put them in order according to season and how often I wear them. I put my shoes in the bottom. It has never chewed my shoes but I don't want to tempt her, plus, it just makes the room neater, to have them up.

What is left to unpack is my dollhouse and my stuffed animals. I think I will always have some of my stuffed animals. I don't so much play with my dollhouse as I decorate it. Momma helped me put tile floors in the kitchen and bathroom of one dollhouse. This dollhouse is the one Momma put together from a kit when I was 3. It has bears in it instead of people. Maybe Em will play with it one day. I put the dollhouse on top of the bookcase and begin setting up the rooms. Momma is calling me. Ms. Jackson is leaving. I and I go back to the living room and say goodbye. Tomorrow is coming.

Momma shuts the door. She is going to make fresh coffee and finish setting up the babies' room. They are fussing, too. I stop to console them. Perhaps we could reposition the baby gate and at least let them roam the hallway.

"Momma, I don't mind if they come to my room. Could we shut your door and the bathroom door and let them wander the hallway? We can put the gate at the living room door."

"That will work. Let me get by with my coffee before you put the gate up. I will shut off my room and the bathroom." Momma shuts those doors and I move the gate to set the babies free. My brother heads to the one door that I am trying to block with the gate. Momma manages to redirect him. The gate is up. Seeing his pathway blocked, he bangs the gate, then sits down and howls in protest.

"I know that you are mad. We will go outside in a little while. Go run down the hallway." Momma throws a ball down the hallway towards my room. He stops crying. Em is looking at the ball. She begins a fast crawl towards the ball. Lars gets up and runs after her. Suddenly, I scampers past both babies, grabs the ball and proudly drops the ball at Momma's feet.

"Good dog, Teacup, you got the ball." Teacup wags all over. Momma throws the ball again. The babies are watching. I hesitates as she comes back down the hall. My brother holds out his hands. "Doggie, doggie. Teacup. Teacup Doggie." T drops the ball in his hands. He looks at it. He throws it. T runs. Again and again. Amazing. T has taught my brother how to play ball with her.

Momma shakes her head. "These are the pictures that we need on camera. We'll just have to remember them and tell them to your father later."

"Momma, when will we see Daddy again? Will they give him some special time to spend with us? It's already been gone a year."

"Honey, I don't know when he'll come or if they will give him some special time with us. But I do know that he will come. Now how close are you to being finished with your room?"

"I was setting up the rooms in the oldest dollhouse. The things for my desk are in a box on the desk. I haven't put books on the shelves. I know where all of my clothes are. Some of my shorts are too short."

"Great work! I'm impressed. I should have had you to organize the babies' things."

"Momma, you are good at organizing, too. You get everything out of storage and into the house, without me."

"Only because you watched the babies. I could not have done it and had them with me. We'll work a little longer and then break for lunch."

Suddenly, the phone rings. We are not expecting anyone to call. Who would know our number? I realize I do not even know our number. Momma and I look at each other. T barks a few puppy barks and then stops. Momma cautiously answers the phone. "Hello," and then she is crying. "Oh, I cannot believe it is you. Finally to hear your voice again, after all this time. Wait, I am going to put you on..."

I do not let her finish. "Daddy, Daddy, Daddy." His voice is filling the room.

"My Precious Tall Child, how I have missed you. I thought I had lost you forever." Daddy is crying, too. My brother begins talking. "Dada, Dada."

Em says "Mama, Mama." She evidently didn't know a daddy. Teacup is barking again.

"Evidently, there have been changes in my family. Somebody fill me in." Momma looks at me. "Daddy, we have a new baby. We go to court about

118

her tomorrow. She's not related to us but she's ours. Someone left her at our door step. Not this house but the other one. Her name is Emily. She's beautiful. We have a dog, too. Her name is Teacup. She's a black, Cocker Spaniel puppy. She came with Emily. And Lars is walking and running. And he can play ball with Teacup."

"Well, that is amazing news. Another daughter and a puppy; Anything else that I should know about? I saw your picture and read the story about you being a hero. I cut it out of the newspaper. It helped me to find you. I love you and your brother and my new daughter. Now, your Mother and I are going to have some time to talk. Hugs and kisses."

"Bye, Daddy, I love you, too."

Momma takes the phone off speaker. Teacup and I go back to my room. I can imagine what Daddy is asking. It is a big surprise to get Emily. If we get to keep her ..., No. We get to keep her. Emily is ours. Daddy will have to put her on his insurance, too. Perhaps he will tell Momma when he is coming home. I and I finish setting up the dollhouse then go outside. Momma is still talking to Daddy in the babies' room.

It feels so good to be outside, to just sit in the warmth of the sun. I have family; I have a home; I have a puppy and we have groceries. Daddy will eventually come home to us, if only for a little while. Tomorrow we will deal with court. It should go even better now that Daddy knows about Emily. I will remember that to discuss with Momma when she gets off the phone.

T crawls into my lap and we sit in the sun, my back against the door. I could bring a cot out here and she could nap. T makes little puppy noises as I stroke her soft black curls. It feels like Momma is watching me. I open my eyes. Momma is at the door.

"You looked so peaceful, I hated to disturb you. Your Dad gave me his phone numbers and his email. You can email him as much as you want. We can't call unless there is an emergency. He will call us back tomorrow to find out about court."

I move so Momma can come outside. "I'm going to get Em and Lars; we'll all come outside." I hear their excited cries as my brother runs down the hall and through my door way.

"Doggie, doggie." He is banging the screen door. I move to the side and open the door. He peeps around the edge of the door. I reach for him and he squeals, laughing, then runs out. Trouses and gives him a puppy bark. Momma comes out with Em in her arms. I move over so that she can sit with me. Momma sits down and turns Em loose. She clambers over to me and rubs her face against Teacup. T thumps her little tail. "T, t, t." Em smiles and crawls off the step. I clap my hands for her.

"Yay, Em. Good talking."

I can't wait any longer. I have to know how Daddy feels about Em. "Momma, Daddy's not upset about Em is he? He's not saying no to Em? Momma, we have to have Em, too!"

"Sweetheart, your Dad is not saying no to Em. You have to realize that taking on a new child, especially when you've just found your family, is a concern. It is a lot to deal with. You can send your Dad pictures of all of us, possibly Ms. Jackson could make us copies of the pictures she took. Men are different than women. They see things in a different way than we do. Let's just get through tomorrow."

"All right, Momma. I'll try. It feels so good to be here. I'm glad that Daddy knows about Em. I don't want her to be a secret. We can let them know in court that Daddy knows about her, too."

Em is crawling around in the grass, pulling leaves off of the plants and wadding them up. Teacup is following my brother. I lean my head against Momma's shoulder. "I love you, Momma. I'm going to check the plum trees for buds.

"I love you, too, Precious. I love you, too."

There are two trees, one on either side of the shed. They are fully leafed out. They don't have flower buds, they have tiny little plums! We can have plums later. Teacup is barking. An older woman with white hair is coming to the fence.

"Hello, are you the new family? What a pretty little dog and these babies are beautiful. You're not going to cut the trees down, are you? They make wonderful yellow, some people say green, plums. Sometimes, there are so many that you have to support the tree limbs so that they do not break."

I introduce myself. "Yes, ma'am, we are the new family. My dog's name is Teacup. This is my little brother, Lawrence and my little sister

Emily. That's Momma coming this way. We are not going to cut the trees down. I was checking them for buds but I see that we have tiny plums. We just moved in. My Daddy's in the Army."

"Well, my name is Ms. Bedford. I've lived here a long time. I always like to have a good back fence neighbor. I hope the trees produce well this year." She stops and introduces herself to Momma. This is my chance to escape.

"Momma, I'll keep an eye on the babies. It was nice to meet you, Ms. Bedford. I am sure there will be plenty of plums to share."

"It was nice to meet you, dear." She and Momma start talking. I head for Em, who looks like she has decided to try and eat leaves instead of wading them up.

"Em, you cannot eat the leaves." She looks at me and spits out bits of green. "Em, that is barfy. Yuck!" I pick her up and check for anything else she may have eaten. She seems OK. Lars comes over. He has a stick and a rock. He offers me the rock and I take it. Suddenly, I have an idea. Maybe Teacup will fetch the stick.

"Let me have the stick, Lars, maybe I will chase it and bring it back." He doesn't quite understand but he gives me the stick. I show it to Teacup and throw it. She watches for a second and goes bounding after it. My brother is delighted. I finds the stick and comes racing back to me. I throw it again. "Me, me, me!" he yells. I hand him the stick. He throws it a short distance. I brings it back. We continue taking turns for several more times. Momma appears.

"Let's go in and make lunch." We each gather up a baby, but Lars wants to walk. Momma gets him over the steps and lets him go. I put the throwing stick on the shelf in the pantry. I put Em down in the hallway outside my room and put the rock on my dresser. Teacup is glad to get to her water dish. Em looks around and starts crawling after Lars.

"Well, do you want leftover pizza and salad or chicken salad?" Momma asks.

"Let's have chicken salad. I'll start Em and Lars off with some fruit pieces after I clean them up." We stop in the bathroom for clean hands and faces.

Once in their highchairs, I give them apple slices and some pieces of banana. I hope Em eats hers instead of smushing them first. I get dishes and Momma gets the food. "Today is special, our first lunch at home. You can have a Coke if you want it."

"Thank you, Momma. I'll have it after lunch, while I finish my room. T and I may nap after lunch, while Em and Lars nap. Then I'll have my Coke. I want to plant our tomato plants this afternoon."

Momma says the blessing. "Lord, we are thankful for each other, for neighbors and friends, for my job and our home. Bless this food to the nourishment of our bodies and us to your service. Look after Daddy. Give us peace in court tomorrow. In Jesus name, Amen." I join her on the amen and the babies clap their hands. T settles herself under my chair. Lars is banging his tray. Em is alternating between eating her bananas and smushing them first.

It is so nice to be able to have something like chicken salad. To sit in a chair, our chairs and have lunch with Momma, not having to have to think about fixing dinner with the cousins.

"Momma, can I start day camp on Thursday or even next Monday? I need time to be here, to just be here."

"Sweetheart, that is fine with me. But I will probably have to go back to work on Wednesday. Let's see how tomorrow goes. I'm not sure I'm ready for you to be here alone."

"I understand, Momma. It was great to hear from Daddy. Kind of like a miracle, our miracle. Everything that has happened lately has been like a miracle.

"Yes, Baby, it has. Now that we have a house, we can be more involved in the church. Are there things you would like to do at the church that you haven't asked about before?"

"There are, Momma, but I want to get tomorrow settled first."

"OK, well, you think about it and we'll have that discussion later. Let's finish lunch, clean up babies and nap."

The chicken salad is delicious. Fortunately, Em has not put mashed bananas in her hair. Mashed bananas might be good for your hair but I don't want to wash hair before we go to bed and nap. Lars seems especially happy and keeps saying "Dada" to no one in particular. We finish lunch. I eat one sandwich and half of another one. Momma volunteers to take Em because she is so messy. Today, I will accept her offer. I put the dishes in the sink and rescue Lars from his highchair. Em breaks into a heart-real tears. Lars is as startled by her reaction as I am. Momma tries to console Em. T begins to howl. I hand Lars to Momma and take Em.

"Em, you are upsetting T. I am not leaving you." I hug Em close as I bend over to stroke T. Em rubs her tears on my shirt and giggles. Lars reaches over and strokes Em's arm. We all head to the baby room for clean up and nap afterwards. Mom and I kiss them both, put them to bed and tiptoe out.

"All right, Sweetie, nap if you want to, stay quiet if you don't. I'm going to nap." She gives me a hug and a kiss. T and I walk down the hall to my room and I shut the door. Peace and quiet in our own space. I put T on the bed. This is all still so incredible. Clean sheets, comfy bed, no quarreling cousins. Teacup snuggles against me and lets out a long puppy sigh. Sleep.

Some time later, I wake up, stretch and turn over. Teacup rouses, and turns over, wagging her tail. She moves from the foot of the bed and comes up close to my face. She stretches back out as I pet her.

"T, we have to get up. We have to finish this room and their are tomato plants that need our attention. Plus, I get a Coke."

T wiggles in happiness. We lay in bed a little longer. We have to get up. I swing my feet over the side of the bed and sit up. I put on my sandals. We are up.

I put all of my books on the shelves, going by size rather than alphabet. It is good to see them on the shelves again, knowing I can read and reread them whenever I want - late at night, early in the morning, before I go to bed, out in the sunshine under the plum tree. T sniffs them all, particularly the lower shelf.

"They are not for chewing, T." She hangs her head and wags her tail. Now for the box of desk things. I set out the brass lamp and the heart shaped clock radio. I set my art supplies at the right hand corner with the wooden figure. I put my journal on the left.

"T, I want to go outside and plant tomatoes. We can finish

setting up the dollhouse tonight." 'T is ready. I listen for noises from down the hallway. Quiet. The babies are still sleeping. T and I tiptoe out the back door.

I set the tomd tomatoe plants along the fence, spacing them out to see how they look. I move them out from the fence a little. They will still grow through the fence and we can share tomatoes with our neighbor. The shovel and trowel are in the shed. 'T is very interested in the holes, and the newly turned over dirt. I decide to dig all of the holes first. It is a little harder than I thought. T starts to dig, her little front paws shooting dirt out rapidly behind her.

"T, you have to stop. That is not helping." Teacup looks guilty and stops digging. I test one of the plants in a hole—not quite big enough. I move T out of the way and make the holes larger. T would fit in a hole. Suddenly, I have an idea! I run back to my room, T at my heels, and grab the camera. I set the the tomato plants in front of their holes and set T in the middle hole, her front paws on the edge of the hole. She doesn't seem to mind. I snap the picture, brush T off, kiss the top of her head and set her down. I center each plant in the hole and add dirt til the hole is filled. We will still need stakes and frames. I wash the shovel and my hands at the faucet at the back of the house. I use a bucket from the shed to water the tomato plants. I can find the hose later. Em and Lars will be able to have a little wading pool.

Momma is at the back door. "Miss Bessie and Ms. Sanders are coming over. Jasper is coming, too."

"Yay! Is she coming to tell us about court?"

"Yes, dear. I know you are worried about court. I am concerned, too." Momma is reading my mind again.

Lars and Em are awake, banging the crib rails and chattering. I can hear them all the way down the hall. T gets a drink, I grab my Coke and we stop in the bathroom. I wash her paws and then wash my hands. Now we are ready for babies.

Momma is already there and hands off Lars to me. I collect toys from this morning and set out new ones. Lars reaches for a truck, not wanting it to be put up. "Mine, mine."

"OK, Lars, we will keep this one out."

"Down."

I put him down. I hope he remembers all the words he knows and uses them tomorrow. Tomorrow. Today could be our last day with Em. Deep sadness. I take Em from Momma, give her an extra hug and kiss the top of her head. The doorbell rings. T barks a greeting, wagging all over. Jasper's deep bark echoes on the porch.

Momma gets the door while I hold Em and hold Lars back from the door. T will be on her own.

"So good to see you. The house has been too quiet without you." Miss Bessie is reaching for Em, Lars and T are trying to get out the door and Jasper is trying to come in. I let Miss Bessie have Em so that I can grab T and Lars. Now they can come in.

"Momma, I am going to let T and Jasper out back. I put a big pan of water in the shade. Em and Lars can just be with us in the living room."

"Thank you, darling." Looking at Ms. Sanders and Miss Bessie, she asks, "Would you like coffee, a soft drink, cake?"

"Coffee is always good. I can't speak for Ms. Sanders."

"I think I'll have a Coke, if that's all right," Ms. Sanders says.

I offer Miss Bessie a stuffed chair with arms by the end table and Ms. Sanders a matching chair by the other end table. Anything set on the coffee table will be fair game for Lars and Em. I settle into the couch with Momma and put toys on the coffee table.

I don't wait for Miss Bessie or Momma to start the conversation.

"I am so glad you are here. My stomach is in knots about court. I've almost finished arranging all of my room. T and I have just planted tomato plants, we've met our neighbor at the back and... and... Daddy called. Momma and I, we talked to him. Lars recognized his voice, too. He saw our story on television! He knows about Em and T. He's going to call tomorrow after court."

Miss Bessie replies, "That's a lot to do and know in such a short time. Child, catch your breath; I'm thrilled that you have heard from your Father. That will certainly help and strengthen our case. Now, let's just talk about court and what happens. We are all focused

126

on Miss Bessie.

"We, minus Jasper, will all come in the morning at 8 o'clock and pick all of you up, including Teacup. Wear Sunday clothes. Court is at 9 AM, but we have to be there early. We can't be late. Try to eat breakfast. Make sure you have all of the baby things. You know that part so much better than I do. When we get there, we will find out which court room and Judge we will have. I think I still know all of them. We will meet Em's attorney; she may want to talk to both of you; Ms. Jackson will also be there. Then... we wait. Sometimes you have to wait several hours before it's your turn. The baliff, the officer in charge of the courtroom will check our names off when we get there and then call us when it is time to go in. The baliff will tell us when to stand, when to sit and when to step forward to the front of the court room." She paused for a moment. "Any questions so far?"

"The baliff duties almost sound like legal Simon Says," I said, smiling slightly.

Lars looked at me and came to stand directly in front of me. "Simon Says." He smiled gleefully and turned back around to hug Em. "Good talking, Lars. Yay for you."

"It is amazing how much that child is talking. I noticed it when all of you first came to stay with us," Ms. Sanders remarks.

"I just hope he won't be shy and he'll talk in front of the Judge," Miss Bessie adds.

"I hope so, too, Miss Bessie." Just talking about court I had to reach out and caress Em.

Miss Bessie continues talking, "When we get into court, in the courtroom, we will walk in and either sit where the baliff tells us to or stand in front of the Judge inside the railing. The case will be announced. The Judge may ask me to speak first, he or she may ask Em's lawyer to speak first. The Judge also gets to ask questions. He or she may even ask to speak with you, dear, in their chambers-like an office or they may spend some time alone with Lars and Em. After the Judge has asked all of the questions they want and looked at the evidence, they will make a decision or ruling on the case. The ruling will be read and then we will be dismissed. Now, do you have any questions?"

"No, Miss Bessie, but it is still scary. I'll try to be calm so the babies will be calm. I'll have you and Momma with me. I can deal with it. As long as we get Em. Do you want to see the outfits I picked out for them and to see the rest of the house?"

"I would love to see their outfits and the rest of the house," Miss Bessie replied. "Ms. Sanders and I have been so excited that you were able to get this place."

I began taking them on a tour of the house. I showed them Lars little blue suit with the frog on the pocket of the coat and the pink cotton dress with the full skirt and slip for Em.

We stood at the back door but decided to tour the backyard last. Ms. Sanders liked the babies' room in the middle. Miss Bessie agreed with me that I had the best room. My curtains did come from her house. We went back through the dining room and the kitchen to the backyard. I showed them the plum trees and the tomato plants. Jasper and I both had dirt on their paws. I let Ms. Sanders and Miss Bessie back in the house and hold the dogs with me so that I can clean their paws. Jasper has really large feet and he kept licking me in the face. T kept trying to get extra attention. Finally, they were clean, enough to come back in. I let them in and hung the towel back in the pantry by the washer and the dryer.

Ms. Sanders and Miss Bessie are getting ready to leave. "We are going to let you good people relax before dinner and tomorrow. Thank you for cleaning Jasper's feet, Child. I know what a job that is. The house looks wonderful. We will be here at 8 in the morning. We love you. Give us a hug."

We hug Ms. Sanders and Miss Bessie and Jasper and let them go. They are to the car when Miss Bessie comes back. "I had a thought. It would be easier if we took Teacup now. Would you mind terribly if T had a sleepover with Jasper?" she asked.

Not have T, not have fuzzy black pup in the bed! Oh, no! But I know Miss Bessie is right. I know that T will have a good time. I know Miss Bessie and Ms. Sanders love her. All of this flashes through my mind at once.

Momma looks at me. "It is up to you, Tall Child," she says, using my nickname.

"All right, Miss Bessie. I will miss her but I know you are right." T is wagging her tail. I get her leash and her food bowl, putting enough food for tonight in a sack. I pick her up, pat her, kiss the top of her head and hand her over to Miss Bessie. T looks back and then prances to the car with Miss Bessie. Jasper is almost rocking the car in his excitement. Miss Bessie puts T in the front seat and then lets her jump to the back. T and Jasper lay down in the back seat. Now it is just me and Momma and the babies. I miss T already. Em is patting my arm and brings me back to reality.

"Yes, Em, my almost little sister, I am still here. Let's help Momma and start some dinner." I hold out my arms and Em reaches for me. I take her from Momma and we head to the kitchen. Lars wants to walk on his own. Momma goes outside and fastens the gate.

Momma and I both want something simple. We fix shell pasta with fresh and canned vegetables, cheese, nuts, steamed chicken and salad dressing. Em and Lars get plain pasta, vegetables and chicken.

After dinner, we sit on the porch. No T to run around the yard. Momma hugs me. "I know you miss Teacup, dear. Do you have everything ready for tomorrow?"

"Yes and yes, Momma. I am still nervous about tomorrow. I think I will just take a shower and go to bed."

"All right, Sweetie. I love you. I'll see you in the morning. Give me a hug."

"I love you, too, Momma. I hope I can sleep without T."

The shower feels good. I stretch and try to let all my tensions wash down the drain. I brush my teeth and listen at the door to the babies' room. Peaceful. My room is awfully quiet without T. I make sure all of my clothes are ready for tomorrow, lotion all of me, turn out the lights and look at the stars. I make sure God knows how I feel about Em. I still sleep on the bed as though T is there.

Morning comes. I awake before the alarm goes off. My hair is still damp; I will put it up anyway. There is no point in staying in bed. We should probably feed Em and Lars before they get dressed or I get dressed. I am so nervous I do not see how I will be able to eat. I hear Momma walking through the house, starting the coffee. I say another prayer about Em and head for the bathroom. Em and Lars are beginning to talk and make noises to each other.

Momma is already in the babies' room by the time I get there. I cannot imagine not having Em. How can I can care so much about a child I have known for such a short time? Em smiles at me and holds out her arms. I scoop her up and hold her close, making sure I will remember how it feels. I kiss her dark, curly ringlets and change her diaper. Momma is quiet, too. She gives me a hug. We move to the kitchen.

Em and Lars are eager to eat breakfast. Momma is having trouble eating, just as I am. I make sure I finish my coffee. We get Lars and Em cleaned up, then we let them play in their room. Momma and I do a quick job of getting ready. One last look in the mirror. Now to help Momma get Em and Lars ready.

It is not quite 8 when I hear Ms. Sanders and Miss Bessie pull into the driveway. I look through the baby bags, everything is there. I grab the car seats while Momma sits on the couch with Em and Lars.

"You look very pretty, dear. I know that you're still nervous. We're all in this together," Miss Bessie says.

"Thank you, Miss Bessie. Good morning, Ms. Sanders. I am still nervous. Did Teacup sleep with Jasper, Ms. Sanders or you?"

Ms. Sanders laughs. "She slept between Jasper's paws on his bed with him. She could have slept with me. I wouldn't have cared."

"I'll be back in a minute."

Momma and I each take a baby and a bag. Momma locks the door. I have my key, too, in Em's bag.

Babies are strapped in and we are ready to go. The drive to the courthouse is short. Ms. Sanders lets us out at the front door. It is a large, old brick building with stone dogs guarding the entrance. It is set back from the street. When we get to the front doors, there is a metal detector and sheriff's deputies just past the doors. Miss Bessie goes first.

"Good morning, Miss Bessie. It is so good to see you again. And look at these fine babies. You folks are in good hands with Miss Bessie."

I put the baby bags on the x-ray machine. I tell the officer about my key.

"Well, young lady. Let's take it out. It will make the detector go off."

I give him my key and walk through holding Em. Lars insists on walking through by himself. The deputies laugh. Momma walks through and we are done.

Miss Bessie goes to find what court room we are in. She comes back and we move to the area outside the last court room. As best we can, we settle ourselves on the benches. It is cold. The benches are hard, with no back or cushions. I am glad that I have a summer sweater and that I put one on Em. Momma and Lars have jackets. Miss Bessie says that we are first. She has given our names to the baliff.

The hallway is full of people - moms, dads, grandparents and babies. Actually children of all ages, but a whole lot of babies and young children. I have never seen so many except at a preschool or kindergarten. Em and Lars are excited; Lars wants to play with the other children. Momma lets him down but keeps him right beside her. Someone is waving at us from the broad hallway. It is Ms. Jackson. She has someone with her, a young woman like herself, with curly red hair.

"Hello, everyone. This is Ms. Carson, Em's attorney."

Ms. Carson smiles. "So this is Emily, what a pretty child you are. Could I hold her? Do you think she will let me hold her?" Ms. Carson reaches for Em. Em pulls her hands in and holds onto me, turning her face away.

"Oh, my, someone is very attached," Ms. Carson says.

"Is that bad?" I ask nervously.

"Oh, no, that is perfectly normal," Ms. Carson assures me. "She doesn't know me and she is obviously very comfortable and attached to you. But the Judge may want to hold her, so be ready."

"I know. We'll just have to see."

Miss Bessie, Ms. Carson and Ms. Jackson all step to the side and discuss the case. It is almost 9 o'clock. I hand Em to Momma and grab a few minutes of solitude, locked in the restroom. I say another prayer and get a drink of water. Momma is standing up when I get back.

"The baliff has just called for us." She hands Em to me and we go in. No turning back now.

It goes just as Miss Bessie said it would. Ms. Carson presents first, then Miss Bessie. The Judge asks Momma questions, then asks to see Lars.

Lars goes willingly. Momma looks at me. We both know that Lars wants to bang the gavel. The Judge comments about how well he walks and what a good size he is. The Judge asks him how old he is, he grins, holds up two fingers and says "Two." Silently, I am cheering for him. The Judge says, "I hear you have a dog at home, a little black dog."

Lars nods. "Teacup. Teacup play ball," he says proudly. Then he reaches for the gavel and looks at the Judge. The Judge nods. Lars bangs the gavel twice. He smiles again. "Down, down." The Judge puts him down. Lars turns and waves. "Bye-bye." He runs back to Momma.

"Well, he seems to be doing fine. His speech is excellent." He turns to me and Em. Em looks at him and turns back to me, tightening her grip.

The Judge asks me about school, my friends, running and the men coming to our garden shed house. I answer all of his questions. Then he asks how I feel about Em. I tell him the truth.

"When we got Em, that first night, I was more excited about the puppy, about Teacup. I was afraid about having Em. I was afraid, if we told the police, they would try to take me away from my Momma. A lot of foster homes do not want older children. I did not want to be separated from my brother. But Em was special. She wanted to be loved. She needed us. She is a beautiful child. She is amazing. I cannot ... I cannot," my voice breaks, "imagine not having her. I love Em as much as I love my natural brother, Lars." I kiss the top of Em's head and hold her close as she cuddles against me.

"May I see her?" the Judge asks.

"She will cry, but yes, you can hold her." I tell Em, "It is only for a moment Em, he will not hurt you." I pry her fingers loose and begin to hand her to the baliff. Em is howling in protest. "No, no, no!"

The baliff takes her. "Come, Little One, the Judge wants to see you."

Em is still reaching for me. Lars is clearly upset. He turns in my Mother's arms and faces the Judge. "No take Em," he declares. "No take Em. Em mine!" He begins to cry.

"My, my," the Judge says, "you have certainly made quite an impression on this family, Emily." He looks at her, dries her tears and tries to get her to play pat-a-cake. Em looks at him, frowning and then joins in.

"Go," she says. She looks back at the Judge, still about to resume crying.

"Bye-bye." She waves at him. He smiles, waves back, says bye-bye and hands her back to the bailiff. She squeals with delight when he hands her back to me.

Then he talks to Ms. Jackson. Finally he asks about Daddy and how he feels about Em. I hold my breath.

Momma answers. "Certainly, sir, he was surprised about finding out about another child in our family, but we had always said we would adopt. Emily was chosen for us and we were chosen for her, by her Mother. We love Em and we want to keep her, forever."

Ms. Carson asks to speak. "Your Honor, I have spoken with Em's Mother and she is agreeable to giving up Em. She voluntarily chose to place Em with this family. She has signed and notarized a letter, giving up custody, her parental rights and asking that Emily be placed legally and permanently with this family. I have also spoken with the Father of these children and with his commanding officers. I can confirm that he also wants this child. The state has no objection to Em being placed legally and permanently with the family."

The Judge confers with Ms. Carson, Ms. Jackson and Miss Bessie. I hold onto Em, turning from side to side with her, kissing the top of her head.

Ms. Carson, Ms. Jackson and Miss Bessie, all move back from the bench and resume their positions. The Judge looks at his papers and speaks."

"Concerning the matter of the minor child, known as Emily or Em, the court, having heard the evidence and testimony of all parties, declares that she" and here he paused, "will remain will remain with the family her Mother chose; her Mother having voluntarily relinquished all of her parental rights. This court will reconvene in 6 months for the purpose of finalizing this decision or amending it. All parties are to return in 6 months, before Christmas."

"Young Lady," the Judge is addressing me, " I commend you for your school grades, for helping your Mother and for accepting Em."

"Thank you, sir, thank you especially for Em."

To my Mother, he says, "Ma'am, the court needs more families who are willing to take in children. I hope you are able to see your husband soon. You have three fine children. I look forward to seeing you in six months. Get your new court date before you leave."

"Thank you, sir. We will be back."

The Judge speaks to Miss Bessie. "It was good to see you, Counselor."

"Thank you, your Honor. It was good to see you and good to be back," Miss Bessie replies.

Em and Lars wave goodbye and say bye-bye. The Judge waves back. Lars reaches and pats Em. "My Em, my Em."

We walk out. Momma has her arm around me. Me and Momma and Lars and Em. And Miss Bessie. We got Em. Outside the courtroom, I am crying in relief. Ms. Carson, Ms. Jackson and Miss Bessie and Momma, are all talking. I sit down and just hold Em, my Em, our Em. Em holds me tight and we rock back and forth.

Miss Bessie comes over and hugs us. "You did an excellent job. Everything is fine. We will come back to court on December 14th." I hug her back and nod my head. Momma comes over and sits beside me with Lars. "We can go home now, Precious. Do you want to wait outside in the sunshine? I'm sure Lars can't wait to climb on the dog statues."

I manage a smile for Momma. We say goodbye to Ms. Jackson and Ms. Carson and head for the sunshine. Momma barely gets outside before Lars is clamoring to get down and climb on the dogs. Em watches for a moment and points, "luh, luh, Lars." She giggles and lays her head on my shoulder. I walk over to the other dog statue and sit down. "Dog, Em, doggie. Big Doggie," I say as I stroke the dog statue. Em reaches and pats it, but says nothing.

Momma comes over. "I think I see Ms. Sanders coming." I look down the street. T is with her. I see a black blur dashing back and forth. She pulls up to the front walk. I manage to grab Lars hand before he runs and transfer him to Momma. We all begin walking, Lars reluctantly, to the car.

Ms. Sanders holds T as Miss Bessie gets in front. Momma and I squeeze into the back with Em and Lars. When we are all strapped in, Ms. Sanders lets T jump in the back with me.

"Yes, T, I missed you, too," I tell her as she covers me in puppy kisses." I lean back against the seat, closing my eyes, holding T, oblivious to the adult conversation. I let go of all my anxiety and nervousness. Peace flows over me. Soon we are home. Ms. Sanders pulls into our driveway.

Still holding onto T's leash, I get Lars out of the car seat and hold his hand. I thank Ms. Sanders and Miss Bessie and tell them goodbye. Momma unbuckles Em while still talking with Ms. Sanders and Miss Bessie. Lars and I walk to the porch while I get my key. He is struggling to get loose. I manage to get the door open and turn him loose inside. I unleash T to follow him. I collapse onto the couch and take off my shoes. Lars and T are running in the hallway. Momma comes in with Em. We are home. Together.

Lars and T come back to join us and we sit on the couch with Momma, enjoying the quiet. The peace of being together as a family.

My name is Lauren Elizabeth and I am no longer Nothingness.